Bhaja Govindam

Bhaja Govindam

Er Govinda Chandra Sahu

Translated By

Pravati Mishra

The Readers Paradise
New Delhi - 110002

Bhaja Govindam

ISBN - 978-93-85958-68-7

Published by
The Readers Paradise
103, 4787/23, Ansari Road,
Darya Ganj, New Delhi - 110002
011-23246222, 23246333 | M. 09654444181, 09312220441
thereadersparadisesales@gmail.com

Printed in India
Balaji offset

Contents

Introduction

Hindu religion faced a crisis when Buddhism started influencing the public mind. At such a juncture the great preceptor of Hinduism, Adi Shankaracharya appeared. He was born in 788 AD in village Kaladi of the state of Keral in south India. By birth he was a Brahmin of the Nambrudi sect. Though Acharya Shankar lived for only thirty-two years he has left an immortal legacy. As the English poet Ben Jonson memorably puts it in 'The Noble Nature': 'In small proportions we just beauties see;/ and in shot measures life may perfect be'. Through his *Bhaja Govindam* Adi Shankar continues to inspires us with eternal wisdom.

The philosophy of Shankar is based on Adwait Vedanta which asserts that brahma is one, the only truth. Brahma is identified with Truth, Intellect and Pleasure. The material world is a transitory one. It is an illusion. Because of man's ignorance regarding knowledge of the self, man in engrossed in the physical world. It is a mistake to think an individual and the brahma as two separate entities. It is brahma, which is recognised as unique and true. Man is a victim of illusion because of his ignorance. During the states of wakefulness, sleep or dream he is under the control of illusion. When he acquires supreme knowledge he realises his own self and receives the supreme pleasure of the brahma.

One day, Acharya Shankar, while walking in the streets of Benares alongwith his disciples, heard that an octogenarian was getting by heart the rules of grammar. He thought that at the time of death such expert knowledge of grammar can never help anyone. Hence Shankar started writing *Bhaja Govindam* or *Moha Mudgara*. Of all his books, this book is relatively shorter, but it contains most useful and moral teaching. In this book the essence of the Vedanta has been presented in simple Sanskrit. The first Sloka is called a refrain. From the second to the thirteenth verse we have twelve noble lessons. These were composed by Shankar himself. The next fourteen verses were composed by his disciples. In the last four verses he had blessed his disciples. Thus, in all, there are thirty-one verses.

Acharya Shankar was upset by the stupidity of human beings and their suffering. To rescue them from misery he explained the inner meaning of the Vedanta in lucid, simple and figurative Sanskrit. The style of his composition is impressive. This book leaves a tremendous impact on human beings.

Man gets ensnared by illusory attachments. He spends his precious life recklessly trying to maintain his proud possessions of wealth, youth, wisdom and power. Being entrapped in such attachments he cannot follow the path of Truth. Before he tries to protect himself from such downfall he slips into the abode of death. Shankar attempted to impart true knowledge about the self through these verses. These will act as a hammer which can demolish all worldly involvements.

This is a unique composition which makes people aware of their suffering caused by desires. It is said in the *Bhagabad Gita :*

विषया विनिवर्तन्ते निराहारस्य देहिन: ।

रसवर्जं रसोऽप्यस्य परं दृष्ट्वा निवर्तते ।। (2/59)

A man can keep himself detached from sensuous enjoyment inspite of his desire for them, but once he obtains an opportunity to derive pleasure in a better way he keeps himself away from carnal pleasures. Such detachment is possible only with the attainment of self-knowledge., At that time desire for earthly pleasures will automatically disappear.

Thus *Bhaja Govindam* or *Moha Mudgar* will enlighten and instruct the readers.

Er. Govinda Chandra Sahu
Plot 1034,
Mahanadi Vihar,Cuttack
Pin-753004
Mob.: 9437411338

Acknowledgements

It is my proud privilege to receive permission from the author Er. Govinda Chandra Sahu to translate his book *Bhaja Govindam* from Odia to English. Going through the Odia text I was enthralled by the simple analysis of the noble lessons offered by the revered Sri Shankaracharya. Er. Sahu's commentary is quite interesting as it contains references to Indian myths, scriptures and anecdotes gleaned from various sources. The message in the book has already spread far and wide through translations from original Odia language into Hindi, Bengali, Sanskrit and Gujurati. It casts light on the great Indian sage Shankar, who had established famous pilgrimage centres in the four corners of our country. Through this English translation of his book Shankar's ideas will cross the boundaries of our state. The book in English translation is expected to reach the English-reading public at large.

At the outset I thank Dr. Jatin Nayak, Prof. in English, Utkal University, Bhubaneswar for the pains he has taken in editing the text. I am grateful to Mr. Ashok Mishra and Mr. Susil Dash for word processing my manuscript. I am thankful to the publisher 'The Readers Paradise' for bringing out the book.

I express my gratitude to my teachers, well-wishers, my friends and family members whose goodwill and encouragement contribute immensely to the completion of the work. I thank Er. Naren Chandra Dash, my husband for his support and encouragement. Last but not the least, I remain indebted to Er. Sahu who encouraged me to translate *Bhaja Govindam* into English.

Dr. Pravati Mishra
'Pranabalaya', At-649,
Mahanadi Vihar, Cuttack-753004
Mob. : 9937083345,
E-mail. : Pravatid@gmail.com

Foreword

The sources of ancient wisdom never dry up and they continue to provide human beings who often get distracted by change and decay, rich, moral and spiritual nourishment. Our narrow concerns and obsessions may conceal them from view but they can always be relied on to give us a sense of direction when we lose our way in a maze of illusions. Learned commentators in every age direct our attention to them and convey the wisdom they offer by expertly interpreting and elucidating it for our benefit. They render the timeless truth embodied in these sacred texts accessible to people living in other times.

This is what Sri Govinda Sahu has done in his excellent commentary on Adi Shankara's *Bhaja Govindam.* This text is located in the context of the everyday experiences of modern men and women and explained with reference to things they know and are familiar with. The task demands not only knowledge, experience and skills of communication but also common sense and a deep understanding of life. Sri Sahu explains the insights of the great sage lucidly and persuasively through stories that appeal not only to our intellect but also to our emotions. Judiciously chosen quotations from the works of well-known Odia poets enlivened and enriched the commentary and illuminate unsuspected facets of Shankara's observations on human conduct and the ways of the world. The reader is exhorted to focus on the higher truths of existence and turn away from transient pleasures.

Sri Sahu has rendered a splendid service to the readers by presenting an extremely valuable commentary on this great book by Adi Shankara.

Dr Pravati Mishra has deftly translated the original and made it highly readable.

Jatindra K Nayak
Professor of English
Utkal University

The Author

Er. Govinda Chandra Sahu is Former Engineer-in-Chief, Water Resources Department, Govt. of Odisha. He graduated in Civil Engineering from the University College of Engineering, Burla in 1963 and completed ME from University of Roorkee in 1976. From 1963 to 2000 he worked for Govt. of Odisha in different capacities from Assistant Engineer to Engineer-in-Chief (Water Resources), in the field of Planning, Design, Quality assurance and Construction of major and medium River Valley projects. After superannuation in 2000, he worked as senior advisor in a Govt. of India undertaking, Member of Task force on Inter-linking of Rivers (constituted by Govt. of India), Chairman Dam Safety Panel, Govt. of Odisha and Member of an expert team for advising Govt. of Gujrat, Tamil Nadu and Andhra Pradesh on dam related issues.

As a writer of repute, Sri Sahu has so far written 13 books in Odia language. He is a recipient of Odisha Sahitya Academy Award (2001). He was felicitated by Odisha Sahitya Academy for his contribution to Odia literature (2004). He is also recipient of Odisha Bigyan Academy Award for popularising science (1996) and was also felicitated by Odia Bigyan Academy for his lifelong contribution to engineering and science (2014). He is editing a thought provoking Odia literary magazine 'The Mahanadi' since 2007.

He has more than 30 technical papers to his credit (13 award winning from Institution of Engineers India, Odisha Chapter) and published three research publications, namely; 'History of Irrigation Development in Orissa' (2009), 'Hirakud Dam Project : Its Background & Performance' (2012) and 'Rengali Multi-Purpose Project : A boon for Odisha' (2014) (All sponsored by INCID,

Ministry of Water Resources, Govt. of India). This is a unique case where both creative literature and technical writing have been nicely blended together.

The Translator

Dr. Pravati Mishra born on 31st Oct. 1948 at Cuttack holds M.A., M.Phil & Ph. D. degrees from the Utkal University, Bhubaneswar. She was awarded diploma 'Nritya Bhusan' for graduation in Odissi Dance from Kala Kendra, Bhubaneswar. After working in Odisha Education Service for 35 years she retired as Principal, Sailabala Women's College, Cuttack. She has authored two critical works - Class consciousness in the novels of 'Kamala Markandaya' (2001) and the 'Early Poetry of Thomas Hardy' (2008). She has translated four collections of Odia short stories into English - 'Snippets of Life' (2006), 'Surrogate Mother' (2009), 'Petals of Joy' (2012) & 'Tears of Darkness' (2012). Three travel books & four children's books go to her credit. For translation she has been awarded 'Odisha Lekhika Sansada Anubada Samman' (2015). For her contribution to literature she has received several awards - Padmabati Samman (2015), Jhumuka Samman (2011), Fakirmohan Smruti Sansada Galpa Samman (2013), Abhipsa Sishu Sahitya Samman (2014), Sukinda Sahitya Samaj Makar Samman (2014) & Mani Manika Sishu Sahitya Samman (2015).

Verse I

Pray to God

भज गोविन्दं भज गोविन्दं गोविन्दं भज मूढमते ! ।
संप्राप्ते सन्निहिते काले न हि न हि रक्षति डुकृञ्करणे ।।
भज गोविन्दम् ।। १ ।।

Meaning - O Dunce !

Think of Govinda, only of Lord Govinda.

When the time of departure draws near, rules and regulations would never be of any help to you.

Commentary - This first sloka is meant to be sung in a chorus. In a religious conference the holy man usually recites a sloka and we sing 'bhaja Govindam, bhaja Govindam'. It fills our heart with love for God driving out lust and worldly desires from us. This first sloka is used as a refrain.

In this sloka, there is a direct attack on human desire for material belongings. Gramatical rules or scientific marvels cannot be one's saviour. One cannot be liberated from this transient world until death. It is written in the *Bhagabat* :

'Death cannot snatch one's life if a fraction of a moment is left.'

In this connection a story from the *Chandyoga Upanishad* is recounted here :

One day Narad, the great sage requested Guru Sanat Kumar to enlighten him as to the Supreme Soul. The Guru asked him, 'What knowledge do you have acquired so far ? After knowing this only can I teach you more.' Narad described in details about what he has learnt. He had mastered applied astrology, mathematics, literature, grammar, art, music and dance. Sanat Kumar said, 'All this knowledge is meaningless, because you have not realized the Supreme Soul. He transcends all this.'

There was a Sanskrit pandit who was proficient in grammar. One day he was going to his in-laws' house. On the way he passed through a dense forest. Evening had set in. Some people at night dissuaded him from going through the forest as it was infested with tigers. They advised him to take rest in a village nearby.

The Pandit said, 'You are stupid. You do not know grammar. How can you know the meaning of tiger? Listen, the term tiger has been derived from a Greek word 'tigris'. The spelling of this word is changed in the French, it is 'tigre'. In Sanskrit it is 'byaghra' which means one who has a strong power of smell. Hence one should not be afraid of a tiger. If at all I meet a tiger in this jungle, it will only touch and smell me. It wont hurt me. That is why I am not scared of taking this road.'

No sooner had the Pandit finished his argument, than a tiger pounced on him from behind a bush. Immediately it tore his throat and drank his blood. At that time he remembers that sometimes in Sanskrit the verb 'ghra' is applicable to eating also. (**घ्राधातुरपि क्वचित् खादनार्थे प्रयुज्यते**) By the time he realized this common knowledge about a tiger he was already dead. Those who boast of their material and useless knowledge of religion and the scriptures, they suffer like this grammarian.

It is true that grammar gives knowledge. It is a means of arriving at a destination. Grammar is essential to understand the deep meanings embedded in the scriptures. But Pandit Shankaracharya opines that it is unnecessary to waste time on earning such knowledge. In order to liberate oneself from the bondage of incompleteness one has to search for true knowledge.

In the Gita it is said,

जातस्य हि ध्रुवो मृत्युः । (2/27)

Man is mortal. It is obvious that whoever takes birth has to die one day or the other. Hence the precious time in which one lives should be spent in unfolding the mystery of the universe. It is said that cowards die many times before their death. It is impossible to escape death. There is a beautiful story about this. One day Lord Bishnu and the Lord of Death were engaged in a conversation. At that time Garuda, the carrier of Lord Bishnu arrived there. Just at that time a house sparrow was flitting from one corner to the other in the house. The Lord of Death looked at that sparrow and looked worried. Garuda took notice of this. He thought that the sparrow was destined to die soon as the Lord of Death had fixed his gaze on it. He decided to save the sparrow from the clutches of death. Hence he took it to a distant island and kept it safe inside the hole of a tree.

Garuda noticed that the Lord of Death was smiling while he was carrying the little bird and again he smiled when he returned and took a long breath thinking that the sparrow was now saved from death. Garuda asked the Lord the reason why he smiled. The Lord replied, 'I was worried as this sparrow was destined to die in a distant island. How would it go there ? When you took it to the destined place i.e. the tree in the island, you helped it not to live but to die. I was apprehending whether such calculation about the sparrow's life would be fallacious. If you did not carry the bird, it could not have arrived at the destined place so soon. You became the cause of its death. By then it was already dead.'

Learning the truth about life and its end Garuda felt quite upset. The Lord said that it is the universal truth; nobody can escape from it.

In order to obtain mental peace, one has to rid oneself of worldly attachments. The only means to attain one's goal is to pray to God. He is the benign soul, the brahma, a conglomeration of the truth, the conscience and celestial bliss. One has to surrender completely to them in order to cross the ocean of the world.

It is said in the 'Mana Bodha Chautisha' –

If you want to be liberated
you have to recite God's name.

--- --- ---

It is useless to take care of the body
Better forsake malice and devote yourself to God.

--- --- ---

Nobody is immortal
Hence sing the name of God
You will be saved.

Lord Krishna has conveyed this essential lesson in a nutshell,

तमेव शरणं गच्छ सर्वभावेन भारत ।
तत्प्रसादात् परां शान्तिं स्थानं प्राप्स्यसि शाश्वतम् ।। (18/62)

This Sanskrit sloka means 'O, Arjun, you surrender yourself to God completely. With His blessings you can attain perennial peace and reach His eternal abode.'

●

Verse - 2

मूढ जहीहि धनागमतृष्णां कुरु सद्बुद्धिं मनसि वितृष्णाम् ।
यल्लभसे निजकर्मोपात्तं वित्तं तेन विनोदय चित्तम् ।।
भज गोविन्दम् ।।२।।

Meaning – Hey, stupid one ! Leave the desire for more wealth. Let nice thoughts arise in your mind. Wealth is like a mirage. Show indifference to it. Be satisfied with whatever you have obtained through your own deeds in your previous life. Be contented with whatever you have earned by yourself.

Commentary : Sarbapalli Radhakrishnan says –

'Wealth, power and efficiency are the appurtenances of life but not life itself'.

Sri Aurobindo said this to his wife, Mrunalini, 'All that education, efficiency, intelligence or prosperity man has acquired is nothing but God's gift. That is why, keep with you whatever you need for maintenance of the family and return the rest to God. If one spends lavishly all these things for one's own comfort and luxury and pleasure it is nothing but a gift.'

How profound is such a thought!
Spending money recklessly is a hateful crime.

Money is at the bottom of all our problems. Too deep an attachment to money brings about one's downfall. How much one may earn, one cannot satisfy his desire for more money. Money can never bring eternal peace or pleasure. Chanakya has warned :

जनयन्त्यर्जने दुःखं तापयन्ति विपत्तिषु ।
मोहयन्ति च सम्पत्तौ कथमर्थाः सुखावहाः ।।

He means to tell us that a man has to undergo much suffering in order to earn wealth. One's mind gets upset if one's property is lost. One feels vainglorious when wealth accumulates. Hence it is obvious that the wealth that causes so much pain in life for its earning, losing and saving cannot give one happiness. It is rightly said in the Kathopanishad,

न वित्तेन तर्पणीयो मनुष्यः ।

that plenty of wealth can never satisfy one. The man who goes on acquiring property is really a fool. Hence it is clear that one can never attain peace unless one abandons one's desire to earn and hoard treasures. The Ishabusyupanishad also says :

तेन त्यत्वेकन भुञ्जीथाः ।

to remain satisfied with one's earnings instead of feeling greedy for others' wealth. In the *Rig Veda* it is said,

महे चन त्वार्मद्रिवः परा शुल्काय देयाम् ।
न सहस्राय नायुताय वर्जिवो न शताय शतामघ ।। (8/1/5)

O' Lord, I cannot give you up for acquiring immense wealth, not even for infinite wealth.

It is universally admitted that wealth is necessary for a man. But one need not go out one's way either to spend money or save it. God is the source of all wealth. If one surrenders to God wealth flows incessantly. Hence try to follow like Nachiketa the path leading to eternal wealth withdrawing one's mind from the terrestrial possessions which can never give one real pleasure.

A mythological story goes as follows : There was a pious and truthful Brahmin in a village. One day, a holy man came there and said to the villagers – 'If the householder answers the call of nature in his kitchen then the faeces will turn into gold. Listening to him most of the villagers did the same except the Brahmin. They lived happily getting easy money from their kitchen. But the pious Brahmin thought that it would be wrong to pollute one's kitchen which is a sacred place for one's forefathers. Inspite of his wife's repeated requests the Brahmin did not change his mind. He said that he would not commit such an impious deed. Finally, the couple decided to leave the village.

They left the village. When they reached the outskirts of their native land the Brahmin said to his wife, 'Let us take a last look at our village where we have spent so many days of our life.' As soon as they saluted their ancestral place and reached the neighbouring village, they saw their own village going up in flames. The village was safe so long on account of the piety of the Brahmin. The villagers' houses were reduced to ashes, destroyed in a moment along with their ill-got wealth.

In this context one of the stories of Leo Tolstoy is worth recounting. Once a king declared that one will win any amount of land that one can cover on foot before sunset. Hearing this a greedy man thought of becoming a big land-owner. He started in the morning. Noon came, then afternoon. He went on covering as much land as he could. Now the sun began setting in the west. His desire knew no bound. He tried to acquire some more land. The audience and the king all were waiting for his return. The sun was setting. The man was dead tired running the whole day. Hence he could not return to the starting point as per the condition laid down by the king. He fell down exhausted. He had to cover only a few yards more in order to return to the starting point. People ran towards him and found him lying dead on the ground.

The king offered a land measuring three hands and a half for his cremation. This was the amount of land all men need for their burial. Thus the story establishes truth that avarice is one of the original sins which leads one to death.

An anecdote about the holy man Purandar is worth citing. He lived in Bijayanagar. At that time Krishnadevray was the king of Bijaynagar. He came to learn about Purandar's simple life and his life of detachment. He could not believe it. Hence he decided to test him.

Purandar lived on alms. The king sent the message through his minister that he wanted to help him by giving him alms daily. Accordingly, Purandar reached the palace. As per the king's instruction, some diamonds and pearls were kept in the rice bowl. The next day the holy man came to the palace. He received the alms with the valuables. The king and the minister thought that Purandar was coming regularly to fetch the valuables. The king knew that Purandar never received alms many times from one house. Hence the king was confirmed about his greed. One evening, both the king and the minister arrived at his house. They overheard the conversation between Purandar and his wife. She was heard telling him, 'To-day also I find some articles mixed with the rice.' She was separating these from the rice. All the valuables were thrown into the backyard of the house. The minister in disguise said, 'Mother, why do you throw away the valuables?' She replied, 'These are real diamonds and gems. These will disturb our devotion to God and our meditations. Hence I am separating these from our rice that we need from the king as alms.'

Both the king and the minister were surprised and felt ashamed. They prostrated themselves in front of the holy man.

Desires know no limits. The more one gets the more one gets dissatisfied. There is an insightful sloka in *Vairagya Shatakam.*

निःस्वो वष्टि शतं शती दशशतं लक्षं सहस्राधिपो
लक्षेशः क्षितिराजतां क्षितिपतिश्चक्रेशतं वाञ्छति ।
चक्रेशः सुरराजतां सुरपतिर्ब्रह्मास्पदं वाञ्छति
ब्रह्माविष्णुपदं हरिः शिवपदं तृष्णावधिं को गतः ।।

This sloka points out how a pauper desires to get hundred rupees. One who possesses hundred rupees, wants one thousand and one who possesses one thousand wants to be a millionaire. Thus man's desire is found to be limitless. A millionaire wants to be a king. A king wants to be an emperor; even among gods there is a competition to be the Lord of Gods. Lord Indra covets the position of Brahma, Lord Brahma longs to be Lord Vishnu and Lord Vishnu desires to be Lord Shiva. Such desires make one unhappy. In order to lead a peaceful life one has to maintain a quiet, detached and satisfied life.

One who never boasts of his riches and spends money

for the needy instead of self-indulgence, is really suitable for obtaining wealth.

The famous Odia writer Fakirmohan sings :–

> O' you rich men, who are swollen with pride,
> tell me how much do you possess?
> The world is a treasure-house
> only a little of it is with you
> you crave for wealth and honour
> your mind must be too weak.
> One who never desires all this
> deserves to be the real owner of wealth.

●

Verse - 3

नारीस्तनभरनाभिदेशं दृष्ट्वा मां गा मोहावेशम् ।
एतन्मांसवसादिविकारं मनसि बिचिन्तय वारम्वारम् ।
भज गोविन्दम् ।।३।।

Meaning – Don't get bewildered at the attracting appearance of women. Get yourself restrained. Don't follow a wrong course. Always think that a woman's breasts and beautiful thighs are only made of flesh and fat. Hence one should restrain oneself against such seductions.

Commentary – Bhartruhari has indicated at the temporariness of beauty and uselessness of carnal pleasure. He said,

'She is not beauty but a desert.
Her breasts are like untrodden hills.
The thief of lust hides these
O' traveller, don't commit mistake in moving there.

All the scriptures are unanimous in advising us to keep away from women and gold, but nowhere neither wealth nor women have been projected as insignificant. Always they warn us against over-indulgence. A man has two needs – one is liberation from sorrows and sufferings; the other one is attaining happiness. Man runs after wealth in order to live safe. He tries to create an imaginary fort around him. The unsurmountable desire for wealth never comes to an end.

After getting satisfied about possession of wealth to certain extent man looks for a woman. Man and woman are beautiful creatures in God's creation. It is natural that a man is attracted towards a woman but there must be discipline, gentleness and holiness in this man-woman relationship. Without discipline man is degraded to the position of a beast.

It is said in 'Hitopadesha' -

आहारनिद्राभयमैथुनञ्च सामान्यमेतत् पशुभिर्नराणाम् ।
धर्मो हि तेषामधिको विशेषः धर्मेण हीनाः पशुभिः समानाः ।।

In the second and third slokas it is repeatedly stressed on abandoning two worthless things i.e. wealth and woman for which man has too much attachment. It is not so easy to give up these things on the part of a weak-minded man. Physical pleasure only leads to sorrows. Hence for real annihilation of sorrows desires are to be destroyed. To realize this a practice with determination is necessary. In the Rig Veda it is said,

अपां मध्ये तस्य वांसं तृष्णा विदज्जरितारम् ।
मृडा सुक्षत्र मृडय ।।

It means that a weak and indisciplined man feels thirsty while standing even inside water. O' Lord, make him happy.

God is wide-spread like water. His pleasure is all pervasive. The nectar flows from Him. One who is engrossed in worldly pleasures cannot realize the taste of nectar. To him nectar appears as poison. One who controls his fascination for material possessions really gets endless pleasure.

A human being cannot get real satisfaction in life as long as he is absorbed in worldly pleasures. He is not aware of the presence of the nectar around him. He feels restless and helpless. All his desires, even after being fulfilled, cannot give him eternal satisfaction.

It is explained through a historical allusion. The story tells us how the King Mahmud of Gajni was able to destroy the Somnath temple with the help of a beautiful temple dancer. The dancer with her glamour spread her destructive charm. The King Bhima and the wretched Shibadarsh were engulfed in her burning fire.

The Somnath temple was surrounded by a fort. There was a beautiful temple dancer whose name was Chola. Shibadarshi was the son of the chief priest of the temple. He was enthralled by her beauty. Chola also deeply loved the boy. Mahmud of Gajni attacked the kingdom of Bhima with many soldiers. The King Bhima had fewer soldiers. They planned to store food-stuff inside the fort. Some soldiers were to fight outside the fort and the others were to shower arrows from inside the fort.

On the first day of the battle, king Bhima pushed back Gajni's forces. On the second day, Mahmud of Gajni gathered the soldiers together and attacked again but got defeated. The king entered into the fort raising a slogan of victory. On the third day king Bhima went outside the fort and killed many soldiers of Gajni. Every body praised the king's valour when he returned to the fort. Chola saluted him saying, 'O' king, when you were fighting you looked like Lord Shiva when He dances 'tandab', a ferocious form of dance. I am overpleased with your courage.' The king replied, 'All this is for you only as I adore your beauty so much.' Chola knelt down and saluted him with reverence and said, 'Sir, this body is yours, I am your servant.'

Shibadarshi was listening this conversation between the king and Chola. He got inflamed. He thought to finish the king so that Chola will be his only. He forgot everything else - his patriotism, and his loyalty. He saw only Chola.

At midnight he sent a messenger to Mahmud. By that time Mahmud Gajni was preparing to go back. The messenger said, 'Sir, you need not return to your land. Today start attacking again. I will show you the secret door into the fort on a condition that you must kill the King and let Shibadarshi sit on the throne.'

Mahmud Gajni got the message. He commanded his soldiers to pass through the gate at night and killed the king's soldiers mercilessly. On the fourth day, when the king went out to do battle he discovered that most of his soldiers were dead. Bhima faught courageously but finally succumbed. When Shidadarshi arrived and introduced himself to Gajni, Mahmud immediately drew his sword and chopped his head. Thus king Bhima and Shibadarshi both were destroyed in the fire of lust for the woman Chola.

Like Shankar, the sage Bhartrihari has said in *Vairagya Shataka* that a woman's body is nothing but a combination of flesh, blood, bone, saliva, sweat and impurities. How is it that poets sing the glory of such a form! Lord Buddha advised his disciples to keep themselves at a fair distance from women. One day, when Buddha was discussing with his disciple, Anand the latter asked,

'How does one deal with women?

'You have to keep yourself at a distance from them.

'Sir, did you see a beautiful girl walking by this road?

'I saw somebody passing this way, may be a man or a woman. I only know that somebody having flesh and bone passed by me.

Hence one should not pay so much attention to something made of bone and flesh. In *Viveka Chudamani* one is advised to overcome one's greed for flesh.

अतोऽभिमानं त्यज मांसपिण्डे ।

In 'Dhammapada' it is said –

यावं हि वनथो न छिज्जति अणुमत्रोऽपि नरस्सनारिषु ।
परिबद्धो मनो व ताव सो वच्छो क्षीर पानो व मातरि ।।

It means that, if love for a woman is not completely destroyed, it is like a calf's attachment to its mother; he is bound by his love for the woman.

One cannot satiate one's thirst drinking salty water. If ghee is poured into fire the flames leap higher. Likewise, desires cannot be fulfilled through more indulgences. This is illustrated by the example of the sage Soubhary.

The sage was taking bath in the Jamuna. He saw a fish couple enjoying sexual intercourse. The sage was mentally disturbed. He thought of ways to satisfy his desire for sex. He went to king Mandhata and told him everything. The king said, 'I have fifty girls. Everybody is beautiful. You can choose any one of them and get married. But the girl of your choice must be willing to marry you.' The king knew that none of his daughters would consent to marry such an old sage.

The sage could read the king's thoughts. Immediately he transformed himself into a handsome young man. He looked quite healthy, youthful and attractive. Not only the princesses but the heavenly fairies would feel drawn to such a man. The sage went to the princesses. All of them were pleased with him. The king was observing this from a distance. He offered all his daughters to the sage.

The sage came back to his hermitage with all the princesses. He made all sorts of arrangements to please the girls. Enjoying his life with the girls, the sage became father of five thousand children. Gradually his lust diminished. He found himself enjoying life no more. Inspite of possessing everything he felt dissatisfied. His mind was full of worries. Now he realized that all his meditations were futile. Although he was an ascetic he forgot his conscience and like the fish couple, indulged in mundane pleasures.

This happened not only to the sage Soubhary but also to Biswamitra and Menaka, to Bharadwaja and Ghrutachi and to Sharadwan and Janapadi. The sages were mesmerized by the beauty of the fairies. Sage Vyasa was born from the union of the sage Parashara and a fisherman's daughter, Satyabati.

Hence it is rightly said in *Manushruti* –

न जातु कामः कामनामुपभोगेन शाम्यति ।
हविषा कृष्णवर्त्मेन भूय एवाभिवर्द्धते ।। (2/14)

The worldly people say that it is difficult to overcome one's attachment to wealth and woman. It is only when one is devoted to the Supreme Soul that such attachment will naturally vanish. One does not want to get worldly pleasures once one avails oneself of that supreme pleasure. Then everything else appears futile. If one's mind is fixed on God all the mundane enticements will be reduced. No more will there be fascination for physical pleasures.

One's wife will share in one's spiritual endeavour. A lotus leaf emerging out of water never catches water drops. Similarly, a man, while leading a worldly life, can live like a saint attaining a free soul.

●

Verse - 4

नलिनीदलगतजलमतितरलं तद्वज्जीवनमतिशयचपलम् ।
विद्धि व्याध्यभिमानग्रस्तलोकं शोकहतं च समस्तम् ।।
भज गोविन्दम् ।। ४।।

Meaning – Like the water drops trembling on a lotus leaf, human life is brittle and temporary. Water is life. Human life is compared with such water bubbles on lotus leaves. This is mortal and temporary. Life is full of sorrows and troubles due to diseases. Man has to realize this truth.

Commentary – How beautiful is the sight of the sun rays over the water bubbles on lotus leaves but it is ephemeral. The bubbles burst when they come into contact with the passing breeze. Human life is like this. Only God knows when all-devouring death would swallow one. Worldly life is full of suffering. The human body is the store-house of diseases. Madhusudan, the Odia author of devotional songs says that nothing is permanent. Life, youth, wealth, water bubbles on lotus leaf all vanish soon. King, subjects, dancers, unhappy men, wise men, wealthy men – all are equal in the eyes of the cruel God of Death. Lord Budha has said, everything is full of sorrows and everything is transitory. A lotus plant grows out of water, takes naurishment from water and finally dissolves in water. The same thing occurs to human beings. Man is like nectar in God's creation. He returns to this fold after death. This world is transient, life is brittle and the body is like a flag that flutters in the wind. Only ignorant people get entangled in the illusory world thinking that such life is permanent.

Bhatruhari has warned us in *Bairagya Shataka* against attaching oneself to the life of transitoriness. Disease, suffering, disgrace, abuse, hopelessness and failure are the constant companions of man. But he never leaves anything behind. A camel while grazing from the thorny plants bleeds, still it is not aware of the injuries. So also is man.

Man grieves the death of his beloved wife. He thinks that his children would become miserable. But, after a few days, he remarries. When his son expires, he feels heart-broken but gradually he forgets his sorrows and engages in worldly affairs. Man becomes bankrupt after giving two or three of his sons and daughters in marriage. Still he wants to have more children. Sometimes he faces litigation over the possession of wealth. But, strangely, a man can neither restrain his desire for wealth nor can he keep himself away from litigations. How strange are the ways of this world! How amazing is man's mind! Instead of breaking free from troubles, man gets himself entangled in them.

Yakhya asked Yudhisthira in the Bana Canto of the epic the *Mahabharat*,

'What is the most amazing thing in this world?'

Judhistir replied,

अहन्यहनि भूतानि गच्छन्तीह यमालयम् ।
शेषाः जीवितुमिच्छन्ति किमाश्चर्यमतः परम् ।।

'Everyday one sees how human beings are dying still they are not aware of mortality. What can be more amazing than such thing?'

Yudhisthira went on :

अस्मिन् महामोहमये कटाहे सूर्याग्निना रात्रिदिवेन्धनेन ।
मासर्तुदर्वीपरिघट्टनेन भूतानि कालः पचतीति वार्ता ।।

This illusory world is like a pan. Lord of Death is trying creatures in this pan with the fire of the Sun, the fuel of days and nights with the help of the utensil of months and years. O Yakhya, this is my answer to your question.

One day a sage came across three people on the road. First one was a prince, the second was a holy man and the third was a hunter. The sage blessed them all. He said to the prince, 'May you live long'. He said to the holy man', 'You may die soon.' Then he said to the hunter, 'You would neither live nor die.'

What is the significance of such different types of blessings? The prince had a lot of money. The sage wished him to live long to enjoy his life for a long time and after his death he would be damned.

The holy man was leading a pious life; hence, if he would die soon, he would be free from suffering and would practice meditation no more. He would go to heaven. For him life and death are the same. There is no difference between this life and the life beyond death.

The hunter leads a dangerous life. He kills living beings. Hence after his death he would go to the hell. There is no difference in life and death for him.

In this ephemeral world death is sure to occur. The wonders of modern science have not obstructed death. If death is inevitable, then why should we not lead a pious and good life? The Bhagabat narrates how to lead a successful life.

तज्जन्म तानि कर्माणि तदायुस्तन्मनो वचः ।
नृणां चेनेह विश्वात्मा सेव्यते हरिरीश्वरः ।।

The life in which man can serve and worship Sri Hari is really a successful life. The work that favours God is the only work. Hence in order to get relief from this mundane world of attachments and illusions man has to meditate on God – this is the only path.

Who knows whether the short-lived flower of life would bloom the next morning? Who knows whether the cool fragrant breeze would blow from the Malaya Mountain? Death is roaming around, an axe in hand. How can we tolerate its hard strokes with our weak bodies ? So, let my lips sing the name of God. Who knows whether in the end it may utter His holy name ?

Verse – 5

यावत् वित्तोपार्जनसत्कस्तावन्निजपरिवारो रक्तः ।
पश्चाज्जीवति जर्जरदेहे वार्तां कोऽपि न पृच्छति गेहे ।।
भज गोविन्दम् ।। ५ ।।

Meaning – As long as a man is capable of earning his kith and kin remain devoted to him. In old age, when his body grows infirm when one cannot make money he becomes unwanted. Nobody likes to take care of him. Hence one should take guard against the situation he has to face in the later part of his life.

Commentary – In this world perhaps there is no one so selfish as man. A man never likes to give anything away unless there is a chance to get something in return. He gives in one hand and expects to get something in the other hand. Day by day we are becoming more and more materialistic and self-centered. As a result, the sacred relationship between husband and wife or son and father or brother and sister is getting tainted. It has turned into a give-and-take relationship. Due to the decay of moral values wealth instead of wisdom and power instead of responsibility are valued more and more. Hence old people are considered not so useful. A man starts growing old from the day he stops earning money. As a result, all his relatives keep themselves at a distance from him. This is the stark reality in this modern society.

The Odia poet of nature, Nandakishore has explained the condition of modern human life in his poems. He shows how human beings turn useless after the end of their capacity to earn.

Now-a-days everywhere one hears the eulogy of money. The rich are known to be sophisticated. They are considered wise and knwoledgeable. As they are capable of giving fat donations they are invited to preside and speak at conferences. They are taken as handsome even though they look ugly. All this is for money only. Now one who is wealthy is accepted as a full-fledged man. As if an abundance of wealth makes man wise, intelligent, eloquent and beautiful.

The famous Odia poet Godabarisha Mohapatra wrote satirical poems. A few lines of his are cited here :

Money !
You can bend a straight thing
Or straighten a crooked one
No body knows how.
You can turn an ugly girl into a beautiful one.
One gets married with your help.
Your other name is bribe
Which works wonders in politics and during elections.

It is true that now a man can purchase everything even honour. If money gives pleasure to man, then it is obvious that one gets unhappy without money. Money is the measuring rod of power, hence one becomes powerless when one stops earning. Money for which a man spends all his time and energy and feels it like a mirage if he fails to find it, in fact brings all troubles to him. Money always harms man. Knowing this man remains blind. After death, this hard-earned wealth is left behind. One's wife cries and comes upto the threshold of the house. The relatives follow him upto the cemetery. The body is burnt and turns into ashes. It is his deeds only that go along with him. That is why it is written in *Panchatantra*.

> द्रव्याणि भूमौ पशवश्च गोष्ठे भार्या गृहद्वारि जनाः श्मशाने ।
> देहश्चितायां परलोकमार्गे कर्मानुगो गच्छति जीव एकः ।।

The Odia poem 'Manabodha Chautisha' tells us :

So many people have left you
Did they carry anything?
You never sing the glory of God
Only indulge in earning wealth.

Wealth never goes with anybody, it is only one's deeds that follow him. Sikandar stopped in Kabul after conquering many places as he fell ill. Inspite of all possible medical care he could not survive. He himself and his minister and other officials were sure that he would die. Sikandar ordered them to bring all his treasures to him. He desired to see these for the last time. Immediately all his wealth was assembled in front of him. He saw diamonds, gems, pearls, gold and ruby and shed tears as he knew all his wealth he had earned by conquering so many countries can never be taken with him. Hence he told his officials to hang his hands on both sides of his coffin which would tell the world that man would leave the world with his empty hands. He had killed so many people, pilfered so much property, but now he had to leave them behind and go empty-handed.

One should learn from such example so that one would not lose heart at times of adversity.

Verse – 6

यावत्पवनो निवसति देहे तावत्पृच्छति कुशलं गेहे ।
गतवति वायौ देहापाये भार्या बिभ्यति तस्मिन्काये ।
भज गोविन्दम् ।। ६ ।।

Meaning – As long as one is alive, friends and relatives take care of him. But once one breathes one's last they call the person a corpse. Gradually, after death the body decomposes. At such time one's beloved wife also keeps herself at a distance.

Commentary – In 'Manabodha Choutisha' the poet says that after death, all that one has earned is to be left behind as one becomes a ghost. Nobody would come near him only six wooden sticks are needed for preparing litter in which the corpse is to be carried to the cremation ground.

In youth a man gets so attached to his body, enjoys his wife and in sickness receives care from his wife, but as soon as he breathes his last, for his wife also his body becomes impure and untouchable. Such is the go of life. Why such false attachment to the body?

Shankar has not forbidden one to have relationship with women. Lord Shiva, Bishnu, Sri Ram and Sri Krishna all were house-holders. Yudhistira, the man of principles had married Draupadi. The sages Jangyabalva, Vedabyasa, Narada and the sage-king Janaka were married. The *shastras* advise people to search for the truth instead of indulging in mundane life. Everything has limitations. One has to keep oneself within limits devoting oneself to the service of God, then one can get celestial pleasure. What is the use of such false vanity for a few days in this life? The famous Odia poet Radhanath Ray tells us that people unnecessarily boast of their superiority to others but, after death, all are equal. It is futile to lead a luxurious life as one has to lie on only six wooden sticks when the soul leaves the body.

Western philosophers criticize Indian philosophers without understanding the meaning of this lesson. They think that Eastern philosophy only preaches pessimism. There is no guiding rule for improvement in life. Such impressions are misleading. The great sages of our country have unravelled the real mystery of life. It is the nature of demons to confine themselves to their own physical existence. Human beings in God's creation have been given a pivotal role as they are intelligent, have conscience, and can judge things in their proper perspective. They have to labour to earn their livelihood and collect things to feed and clothe themselves. They manage their household. All this is necessary. This does not mean that we have to spend all our time in taking care of our body only.

There is a mythological story. In the war between the Kaurabas and the Pandabas many people died at Kurukshetra. Vyasadeba mourned the demise of his progeny. He decided to go far away from the battle-field. On the way he saw one spider who was running away to save its life. Vyasa asked him the reason of his flight. The spider hastily climbed on an ant hill on the other side of the road and said, 'O' sage, don't you know that Arjun's chariot will pass by this road? If by chance one falls down under the wheels, is it possible to remain alive?'

Hearing this from the spider Vyasa laughed. He said, 'Every day thousands of soldiers are sacrificing their lives. For a small creature like a spider, who will cry? Nothing will happen when you die.'

Hearing this, the spider felt hurt. He said, 'Why do you think like this? You are a learned man. I have my wife and children. They are my near and dear ones. My life is quite valuable for them. If I die they will also cry. The death of our kith and kin overwhelms us with grief. Like human beings we also feel joys and sorrows. We have also attachments and affections'.

Vyasadeva thought that such attitude to life is universal. Man is the highest creation on account of his conscience and powers of thought. This is the significance of man.

All animals, birds and insects can be compared with the sea and man with a speedy flowing stream. A stream is small and narrow but its water is sweet and satisfying. On the other hand, the ocean is vast but its water is salty. What is the mystery behind this? With a little thought this mystery can be unravelled. The stream collects water and flows towards the sea. It merges with the sea. But the ocean only receives water. It never gives away water. Hence the water stored like this becomes salty. Human beings should learn from the example of the stream. As the best creation of God, man should perform his duty towards society, not only for himself. Then only he can attain divinity.

●

Verse – 7

बालस्तावत् क्रीडासक्त: तरुणस्तावत् तरुणीसक्त: ।
वृद्धस्तावत् चिन्तासक्त: परमे ब्रह्माणि कोऽपि न सक्त: ।।
भज गोविन्दम् ।। ७ ।।

Meaning – One's childhood is generally spent in playing games. During youth men are attracted towards beautiful women. In old age men get extremely worried suffering from worldly problems. Thus, in one's whole life one does not get the time to concentrate on the Supreme Soul.'

Commentary – The saint Yashobant has reflected on such issues :

You are not chanting the names of
Rama, Krishna and SriHari
Your ten years were spent in frolics
In the twelfth year you begin to cover your self with clothes.
But you had no time to think of God.
Your youth has been spent with your spouse
Never did you chant the name of God
How would you cross the ocean of this world?
Your end is drawing near.
Think of the life beyond this life.

Man is mortal. He has miles to go before he sleeps. The path is full of thorns. He is capable of making impossible things possible. He can easily attain divinity. But it is strange that instead of awakening his inner potential he is running after illusion only. Everybody is running after the unreality. Desires and aspirations trap human beings in a cell.

It is natural that a boy likes to play. Man gradually passes through stages of adolescence and then youth. During youth he dreams sweet things in life and builds castles in the air. He runs after money and women. He becomes disillusioned. sages even get enchanted.

One day, Krishna and the sage Narad were travelling together. On the way Narad asked, 'What is the real nature of illusion?' Krishna kept silent for some time, then said, 'I am feeling thirsty. Can you get water for me?' Narad immediately went to fetch water. He went to a house and knocked at the door. A woman opened the door. She was so beautiful that Narad instantly fell in love with her. He forgot about fetching water for Krishna.

Narad married the woman, became a householder. He fathered children. After a few days there was a heavy flood in the village. Everything was swept away. Narad ran along with his wife and children to escape the flood. But in the heavy rush of water his wife and children were lost. Narad felt bereaved. He cried aloud. To his surprise he saw Krishna appearing before him. Krishna asked for water. Now Narad could realize his mistake. He prostrated himself on the ground and prayed, 'O' Lord, please rescue me from such illusory attachments.'

Thus spending one's youth one faces old age. The evening of life is the right time to surrender oneself at the feet of God. Once a man asked the sage Kabir, 'Sir, How can I see

God?' Kabir kept silent for sometime. When evening fell he said, 'See how the sun is going to set.' Hearing this that man saluted Kabir and then went away.

Others who were sitting there wondered why Kabir answered the devotees' question like this. Kabir replied that he had given the right answer. People followed that man and asked him if he was satisfied with the reply that Kabir gave to his question. The man said, 'Yes, my life is advancing towards its end. My teacher advised me to shed my worldly attachments and devote myself to God.

A similar incident happened in the life of the great sage Raman. Once in Andhra a young man came to see Raman Maharshi. He asked, 'O Lord! I want to learn about salvation. I have read a lot on the Vedanta. I have consulted many monks and sages. Each showed me a different path. I could not decide which one is right. Hence I have come to you.'

The sage smiled and said, 'O.K. You have to go back as you have come.' The devotees present there laughed. The young man felt confused. He waited until the sage Raman left the room. Then he said to others, 'See, how I have forsaken all my comforts and come to learn something about salvation, but the way the sage treated me, is it not an insult to me?'

One of the devotees said, 'No, he did not mock you. This is the right answer. The proper knowledge about salvation is to realize who I am. You asked about the path, and he said that it was the right path. Hence you have to follow this path that you have adopted. Then only you can attain salvation.'

●

Verse – 8

का ते कान्ता कस्ते पुत्रः संसारोऽयमतीवविचित्रः ।
कस्य त्वं कः कुतः आयातस्तत्त्वं चिन्तय तदिह भ्रात ! ।।
भज गोविन्दम् ।। ८।।

Meaning – Who is your beloved wife? Who is your loving son? Who are they, your son, wife and daughter for whom you are so much worried? Who are you? Where from did you come to this world? This world is certainly very wonderful. You have to ponder seriously about the real truth instead of getting swayed by illusions.

Commentary – Man is a social being. He is bound by family ties. Through these his personality develops. In a family he has to live amidst his relatives like his parents, children, brother and sister, wife and friends. In doing so his selfishness and self-centeredness get reduced. Getting married men and women become parents. Thus, gradually a human being, receiving family love and affections, floats in an illusory world. He gets entangled in worldly cares. Shankar tells us of ways of breaking free from such bonds.

The woman whom you love so deeply what actually is she to you? What is your son to you, who is dearer to you than your life?

This world is as wonderful as mysterious. Where from did you come to this world? Where you were before you came here? Did you achieve your own identity? Did any one contribute anything to it? What are your relatives to you? Who are so dear to you? Why are you so worried for them? If you closely analyse this, your wrong notions would be removed and you will get peace of mind. One can realize the difference between this brittle world and the eternal soul.

In this life everybody has a different time of birth and death. We are like passengers in a train. Once we arrive at our destination we have to get down. Likewise, after we finish our work, we have to depart from this world. Nobody waits for anybody else.

First you have to think about your relationship with your children. Only after one takes birth one becomes a son. He was a foetus before birth. Before that he was a sperm. The seed is nurtured by food. Food is available from the earth. Thus the origin of everything is soil or earth. After death, our body dissolves in the soil. Hence life starts from the earth and returns to it. It is the mystery. It is illusion.

One day a stranger came to Lord Buddha to enquire about himself. Buddhadev wanted to test him to find out how much he was really interested to know about self. The next day he gave him a plate full of water. He was instructed to move round the city holding that plate of water. He was instructed not to drop a single drop of water from the plate. After returning he had to tell Buddha what he had seen in the city. Buddha told one of his disciples to follow the stranger holding a sword. He had to cut off his hand if at any time a single drop of water fell on the ground.

All the city men anxiously watched the stranger walking, a plateful of water in hand and a soldier following him holding a sword. The man who was holding the water pot was silently watching the plate. They returned in the evening and met Lord Buddha. Buddha asked him about the city. But the stranger could not tell him anything about the city. He said, 'I concentrated on the plate of water only, I was afraid of the sword. Please forgive me.'

Buddha said, 'Now you are eligible to learn about the self. The noise and decorations in the city could not disturb your mind. You will be able to acquire knowledge about the self after showing that you are capable of concentration. Remember, this is the path that I show to my disciples.'

Every object has two aspects – one is coarse and the other one fine. The tree inside the seed is not visible. Once the tree comes out of the seed, the seed disappears. It is obvious that the seed exists in the tree or the tree was inherent in the seed. Exactly like this, the soul exists inside the body. The soul is so fine that in order to know it, the finest type of power is necessary. That is knowledge of the soul. It is possible through the intellectual vision.

In ancient times there was a king named Khatwang who belonged to the dynasty of Surya. He was a very powerful king. Once the Gods were overcome by the demons and took shelter in the king's court. Khatwang conquered the demons and assured the Gods of their safety. Indra, the king of Gods, was pleased. He offered a boon to the king. The king was not willing initially to ask for a boon. He asked to give him knowledge about the span of his life. To his surprise, Indra said that he would live only for one moment more. Khatwang said, 'O Lord, I am not begging from you a long life nor a luxurious life. I believe that it is better to be burnt in an instant than to remain a putt of smoke for ever.' In the *Mahabharat* it is said,

मूहूर्त्तं ज्वलितं श्रेयः । न तु घूमायितं चिरम् ।।

The famous Odia Poet Radhamohan Gadanaik says :

It is better to die early doing noble deeds,
A long life without worth is of no account in this world.

I don't want to be trapped by this cycle of birth, death and again birth. I wish I would get knowledge of the self and the life celestial. Lord Indra granted him his wish. The king sat in meditation and left his body.

The popular Odia poet Kuntala Kumari Sabat has written a poem developing the same idea :

Who is father, who is son
who is mother?
It is only in inllusion
Once the illusion is shattered
everything is void.
Illusion entangles us
like chains.
Father, mother, brother and
sister – even husband and wife–
All are chained by illusions.

●

Verse – 9

सत्सङ्गत्वे निःसङ्गत्वं निःसङ्गत्वे निर्मोहत्वम् ।
निर्मोहत्वे निश्चलत्त्वं निश्चलत्त्वे जीवन्मुक्तिः ।।
भज गोविन्दम् ।। ९ ।।

Meaning – If one remains in the company of pious people, one feels gradually detached from this world. Because of this detachment illusions about the world evaporate. Then the mind becomes quiet. In tranquility only the supreme soul can be realized. As a result, one attains liberation.

Commentary – Sage Bhartrihari has written in *Nitishatakam* about the value of enjoying the company of holy people.

को लाभोः गुणिसंगमः किमसुखं प्राज्ञेतरैः संगतिः
का हानिः समयच्युतिर्निपुणता का धर्मतत्त्वे रतिः ।
कः शूरः बिजितेन्द्रियः प्रियतमा काऽनुब्रता किं धनं
बिद्या किं सुखमप्रवासगमनं राज्यं किमाज्ञाफलम् ।।

If one remains in the company of wise men
What else one needs in this life?
If one befriends a foolish man
It becomes the root of all his troubles.

Hence it is advised that one should shun the friendship of evil-minded people as they are more poisonous than serpents. It is said, 'A man is known by the company he keeps.'

When a glass comes in contact with gold it shines like a

gem. Likewise a dull man is enlightened coming in contact with wise people.

काचः काञ्चनसंसर्गाद्धत्ते मारकतीं द्युतिम् ।
तथा सत्सन्निधानेन मूर्खो याति प्रवीणताम् ।। (Hitopadesh 42)

Friendship with holy people is like the relationship between milk and water. It is unbreakable and inseparable. When water is mixed with milk, it loses its existence as a separate entity. When milk is heated, the water level decreases and then milk feels sorry for its friend and boils over the pot, falls into the fire. If again water is mixed with milk, then milk feels satisfied. Holy people have a sacred bondage with one and all. They rescue people from pitfalls whereas bad company always drives one to a fallen state.

Shankar has taught us how to climb steps one after another in order to reach the top. With holy company man raises his mental level and loses interest in worldly affairs. One gets distanced from attachment one feels anxious to arrive at divinity. Thus one achieves liberation in life.

The *Gita* fills us how a man reaches a lower level spiritually in second chapter,

ध्यायतो विषयान् पुंसः सङ्गस्तेषूपजायते
सङ्गात् सञ्जायते कामः कामात् क्रोधोऽभिजायते ।
क्रोधाद् भवति सम्मोहः सम्मोहात् स्मृतिविभ्रमः
स्मृतिभ्रंशात् बुद्धिनाशो बुद्धिनाशात् प्रणश्यति ।। (2/62-63)

A man is easily attracted to something sensuous. Desire crops up from sensuousness and then anger. Wrong conceptions arise out of malice. Then one suffers from forgetfulness, which pulls him down. Finally, one gets lost.

A man comes in contact with many people. He has to take help of his conscience about selecting his company. If by chance one falls into bad company his life gets corrupted. In good company only can one achieve spiritual uplift.

Once Narad asked Lord Vishnu, 'O God, please tell me what benefit do we get out of associating ourselves with good people?' Lord said, 'You have to go to a forest now. A black bee is residing inside the hole of a big tree. That black bee will answer your question.'

Narad went to the earth and reached that tree. He saw the black bee humming and flying about. As soon as Narad saw him the black bee fell down dead. Narad came back to Lord Vishnu and told him what had happened. This time Vishnu sent him to a village where a cow had given birth to a calf. He would get the answer from that calf.

Narad immediately went to that village and heard that actually a calf was born there. But as soon as he saw the new-born calf it died. Now Narad felt guilty thinking as if he was responsible for the death of two creatures. When he said this to Lord Vishnu, God consoled him telling that whoever is born has to die. There is no need to get perturbed about it. Finally, Narad was told to go to another village where a male child had taken birth.

Narad went to the village and was informed about the new born baby. He was pleased to see that the baby was quite healthy. He fell compassion for the baby. He thought that he should not be the cause of this death as it had happened in case of the black bee and the calf. He decided not to see the baby. Just when he turned back he heard the sound of a new-born baby who was calling him to listen to him. He said he would give him the answer he wanted to get from God. The baby said that he was a black bee in his former birth and the calf in his previous birth. Because he got the company of a holy man like Narad, he could be freed from those two previous births and now is blessed with human life. He was obliged to Narad as he was born as a human being so quickly because of his contact with a holy man like him.

Narad was now satisfied. He had got his answer. He continued playing on the Veena and went back to heaven.

Sri Ramkrishna narrated a story which is worth recounting here. There was a monk in a hermitage. A prostitute stayed nearby. Many people came to her house. The monk blamed her for her sinful actions. He kept warning her that after death she would surely go to hell.

The prostitute repented for her misdeed but she was helpless. She had to earn her livelihood.

The monk placed stones to keep a count of the people visiting to her house daily. After some days there was a heap of pebbles. One day the monk called the prostitute and told her about the magnitude of her sin. The woman felt offended. She prayed to God to free her from such a life. That night she died. The monk also breathed his last that night.

The followers of the Lord of Death came and carried the soul of the monk to hell. The followers of Lord Vishnu came and took the soul of the prostitute to the abode of Vishnu. The monk shouted, "How is it that the prostitute will be carried to heaven and the monk to hell?"

The followers of Vishnu explained to him that, as the woman repented for her misdeeds, her soul became purified. That is why she was carried heavenward. But the monk was always thinking of the prostitute, hence he was carried to hell.

This shows how the company of holy people gives tranquility to mind. The soul becomes purified. Holy men are our guardians. No one can attain devine grace without their company. Saint Tulsi Das has said this in the *Ramacharita Manasa* :

> Without a holy man's contact
> No conscience can be refined
> So also without Ram's will
> No one can obtain a liberated life.

Verse – 10

वयसि गते कः कामविकारः शुष्के नीरे कः कासारः ।
क्षीणे वित्ते कः परिवारः ज्ञाते तत्त्वे कः संसारः ।।
भज गोविन्दम् ।। १० ।।

Meaning – When one's youth is spent, the power of a man decreases. No more does he feel the pangs of desire. When a pond dries up it looks dull. So also nobody comes to a man, when he loses his wealth. His family becomes unbearable for him. Once he achieves knowledge about the self, he easily knows the uselessness of this worldly life.

Commentary – Human life is short. Youth is one of the four stages in man's life. How long can it last? During that short period man thinks himself a conquerer and does not care for anything. The famous Odia poet Kuntala Kumari has pointed out its dangerous consequences :

Look at the flower '*palasa*' (Butea monosperma)
It has no scent
The same is true of human youth
It is like bubbles, which vanish quickly
Gold is quite deceptive
Hence do not see it as a friend
Rather it is one's foe.
Hence don't get disillusioned.

A Sanskrit sloka tells us that, after a lamp is burnt out, it does not need oil. Once the thief goes away stealing from house, it is useless to practice caution any more. After youth passes away, the company of a wife is redundant. After water dries up in a pond it is useless to build a dam.

निर्वाणदीपे किमु तैलदानं
चौरे गते वा किमु सावधानम् ।
वयोगते किं वनिताविलास:
पयोगते किं खलु१ सेतुबन्ध: ।।

(Subhasita Ratnabhandagaram)

According to Shankar, if there is no work how effect will be generated? To understand this eternal truth one needs knowledge of the self. The story of Nachiketa is recounted here to understand self-knowledge. Once sage Bajastrabana was performing a sacrifice. After it was completed he donated all his wealth. Then he gave away sacrificial fee. It was a sickly old cow. Nachiketa was his only son. He did not care for such insignificant fee. Suddenly it occurred to him that after the sacrifice was over he would give up everything. 'I am his son. If he does not donate me his work will be half done', he thought. Hence he asked his father who he would give his son to. The sage angrily said, 'I give you to the Lord of Death.'

Hearing this Nachiketa was surprised but as his father had offered him to the Lord of death he started towards the realm of Death. The door was closed as the Lord had gone out. He would come after three days. Nachiketa sat waiting for him there without food or water or sleep. The Lord came back and saw a Brahmin waiting for him. He said, 'I have. committed three mistakes by keeping you hungry. You may beg three boons from me.'

Nachiketa was pleased. He said, 'O my Lord, as I have left my father, he is grief-stricken Please give me that boon by which my father would meet me and his sorrows would be removed.' The Lord was surprised to find that Nachiketa not begging for wealth. Nachiketa said, 'Wealth is the root of human misery.' Please give me that knowledge with which God remains happy. God taught him that hymn. God said, 'So far no body has been my disciple, you are my first student. Now you can ask for the third one.'

Nachiketa said, 'O' Lord, please explain to me the mystery of the soul. Where does it go after death?' Lord of Death said, 'This secret hymn Gods don't know. Instead of this hymn, you can beg whatever wealth I can give to you, even your immortality.'

Nachiketa's mind was pure. He said, 'O Lord, I do not need anything else. I want the mystery of death. Please give me that knowledge of self.' The Lord was overpleased looking at the boy's strong mind and desire for knowledge. 'He said, 'Nachiketa, you are the first person to get wisdom from me. Now you go back to your father as you have received knowledge.' In due course, Nachiketa the learned became a great seer who could conquer death.

All human activities are divided into two sections – one is auspiciousness and the other is our likes. All kinds of enjoyment is derived from our fascination for the likes. Man runs after this only. His time is spent in satisfying his desires. Where is time to think of the greater way! But sometimes it happens in other ways. There are some wise people who advance along the path of truth, justice and religion. Yoga and spiritual thoughts are the best ones. This removes the ego from one's mind. Enjoyment, desires all vanish. The truth is revealed and ego is conquered. He knows the Brahma. Hence when there is still time adopt this auspicious course of truthfulness and righteousness.

It is said in *Vairagya Shatakam* –

यावत्स्वस्थमिदं शरीरमरुजं यावज्जरा दुरतो
यावश्चेन्द्रियशक्तिरप्रतिहता यावत्क्षयो नायुषः ।
अत्मश्रेयसि तावदेव विदुषा कार्यः प्रयतो महा-
न्संदिप्ते भवने तु कूपखननं प्रत्युदमः किदृशः ।।

As long as one enjoys sound health
Old age is far away
If one has not neared old age
The sense organs keep fit.
But for spiritual uplift
This is the fittest time.
When health deteriorates
What can one do for life?

The famous Odia poet Fakirmohan has said,

Both conscience and desire
hold humans tight.
Wise men only can think
And accept the rule of
conscience and others
cling to their baser desires.

Verse – 11

मा कुरु धनजनयोजनगर्वं हरति निमेषात् कालः सर्वम् ।
मायामयमिदमखिलं वुध्वा ब्रह्मपदं त्वं प्रविश विदित्वा ।
भज गोविन्दम् ।। ११ ।।

Meaning – Wealth, human life and youth all are temporary. Never boast of this. Time devours all in a moment. All this is pure illusion in the world. Hence realizing this, one should try to attain the state of Brahman.

Commentary - The poet, Madhusudan says :

Pride, ego all vanish in a moment
Like dreams in sleep
Time devours all pride and ego
like bubbles.
Wealth, vanity and ego whatever
one earns in life
vanish so quickly.

Wealth, prestige, family relations and unsurmountable youth – all are vanishing. All this only draws us towards pleasure. It has been already mentioned how distressing is the result of desires.

Wealth and enjoyment pull a man downward. These are worldly desires, which are fulfilled easily. Man is the best creature in God's creation. If man is elevated to the state of divinity, Gods become envious. That is why Gods attract man towards wealth.

The causes of human downfall are – desire, anger, greed, malice, drinks, idleness and sleepiness. Man suffers a lot when he is under the spell of any one of these. His happiness is kept at bay.

It is said in *Hitopadesha* -

यौवनं धनसम्पत्तिः प्रभुत्वमविवेकिता ।
एवैकमप्यनर्थाय किमु यत्र चतुष्टयम् ।। (11)

Youth, wealth, mastery and dullness – each of these leads to destruction. What would happen to one who acquires all these four?

There is a Greek story. Many visitors come to a sphinx. They are bewildered looking at its smile. Once a man asked for riches. The Sphinx assured his prayer but laughed. That man became rich, got proud of his riches. Gradually, his other affections, love and good qualities vanished. He desired only for more wealth. He was obsessed with thoughts of wealth only. Now he realized why the Sphynx had laughed. He was now a captive of wealth.

Another man prayed for a beautiful wife. The Sphynx fulfilled his desire. That woman was unfortunately a bad one, very cruel and strong willed. The man lost all his love and affection. He realized why the Sphynx was laughing. The physical beauty was only deceptive.

Another man wanted to be established in society. Sphynx laughed and fulfilled his desire. He became famous in society. Many people came to him day and night. As a result, he could not find time for his wife and children.

Gradually, his relation with his family got strained. He realized that fame and reputation would not give real pleasure in life. It was, in fact, an illusion.

If one wants to remain happy one has to keep oneself detached from the worldly deceptions. One approaches death as quickly as he is nurturing desires. Thus one is pushed into misery and helplessness. Sage Bhartrihari has explained in the *Vairagya Shatakam*.

एतस्माद्विरमेन्द्रियार्थगहनादायासकादाश्रय
श्रेयोमार्गमसेशदु:खशमनव्यापारपक्षं क्षणात् ।
स्वात्मीभावमुपैहि सैत्यज निजां कल्लोललोलांगतिं
मा भूयो भज भङ्गुरां भवरतिं चेत: प्रसीदाधुना ।।

Its translation into Odia language by Janakiballav Patnaik means to depict :

Keep yourself away
From pleasures of the organs
This world is full of woes,
Hence adopt the right path.
Make friendship with the
Real friend of the soul
Concentrate on eternal
Soul as this world is ephemeral.

One day Goddess Laxmi asked her consort Vishnu, 'O Lord why is it that your devotees are poor ?' The Lord replied, 'See my dear Laxmi, wealth is the cause of all misery. By acquiring wealth man becomes prey to attachments, ego and vanity. All this creates obstacle on the way to liberation.'

In order to test the truth of such a statement Laxmi and

Vishnu appeared in the guise of an old Brahmin and his wife. They went to a rich man's house. They saw people engaged in prayers, incantations and songs. The rich man had smeared sandal paste on his forehead, wore a garland of 'rudrakhya' and was chanting the name of God. In his house there were hundreds of milking cows. The old couple called 'Ma, Ma' loudly. The mistress of the house came out to see the strangers. They begged her for milk to drink. The lady scolded them pointing out their idleness. The old man said, 'Mother, I am sick. That is why I was expecting some milk from your house." The lady gave them curd and ghee as milk was kept for the Puja. The Brahmin drank curd and blessed the donor with thousands of cows.

Then the old couple went to a cottage situated on the outskirts of the village. There lived a man, his wife and their son. Both were great devotees. They kept a cow in the front side of the house. The old couple begged for food, the mistress of the house came out. She immediately invited them to come in. The householder came and said that their cow gave only a half litre of milk. They met their family's need with this. He said, 'You are sick, hence your need for milk is greater than ours.' The Brahmin drank the milk and blessed them saying that their cow should die. The householder was happy at this as to manage a cow was very difficult. Lord Vishnu explains to his consort, 'Now without a cow he would get sufficient time to engage himself in good deeds but that rich man will be more and more engaged in household work, as he will get more cows. Gradually he will forget me and will be engrossed in worldly activities'.

●

Verse – 12

दिनयामिन्यौ सायं प्रातः शिशिरवसन्तौ पुनरायातः ।
कालः क्रीडति गच्छत्यायुस्तदपि न मुञ्चत्याशावायुः ।।
भज गोविन्दम् ।। १२।।

Meaning – Night comes after day, morning after evening, spring and then autumn, like this the seasonal cycle goes on. In this cyclie the human life-span decreases and he advances towards his end. Still then man's hopes and desires never cease, rather, they go on increasing. This is really a thing of wonder.

Commentary – As soon as night appears the day comes to an end. With sunrise night vanishes. Noon, afternoon and evening follow automatically. This is the rule of the universe. A common man cannot understand how each sunrise and sunset snatch away one day from his life. One who has not realized the value of life and is engaged in material pleasure and wife, his conscience has not been awakened yet. He cannot know how his life-span decreases day by day and only valuable time is wasted.

आयुर्हरति वै पुंसाम् उद्यन्नस्तं च यन्नसौ ।
तस्यर्ते यत्क्षणो नीतः उत्तमश्लोकवार्तया ।।

(Bhagabata-2-3-17)

It means that man's life lessens with daily sunrise and sunset. But one who spends his time in praying to God and thinking of God, his life-span is not affected by sunrise and sunset.

Time passes on. It waits for none. The present moment becomes past tomorrow. How soon a man crosses various stages in life – childhood, adolescence, youth and finally, old age. As much as one grows, death comes nearer. This Nachiketa had realized. He said to the Lord of Death, 'Even if you give me more time to live it is not immortality.' It is said in the Upanishad:

अपि सर्वंजीवितम् ।
अल्पमेव वाहास्तव नृत्यगीते ।

Bhartruhari has analysed this in *Vairagya Shatakam* :

आयुर्वर्षशतं नृणां परिमितं रात्रौ तदर्द्धं गतं
तस्यार्द्धस्य परस्य चार्द्धमपरः बालत्ववृद्धत्वयोः ।
शेषं व्याधिवियोगदुःखसहितं सेवादिभिर्नीयते
जीवे वारितरङ्गबुद्बुदसमे सौख्यं कुतः प्राणिनाम् ।।

If man lives for a hundred years, half of it is spent in sleep. From the other half again half is taken up by childhood and old age. A lot of time is spent in battling diseases, sorrows and hopelessness. Human life is as evanescent as water bubbles. How can one find real happiness? Bhartuhari has explained further the impermanence of life. He says that we really don't enjoy anything in life rather our desire enjoys us. We do not know how time is fleeting. Our age and our desires are never satisfied. It is our physical being that decays soon.

भोगा न भुत्का: वयमेव भुत्का:
तपो न तप्तं वयमेव तप्ताः ।

कालो न यातो वयमेव याता:
तृष्णा न जीर्णा वयमेव जीर्णा: ।।

According to Buddha, desire is the root cause of all our sufferings. For this irresistible desire only man gets reborn and endures sufferings. Aspirations, one after another, trouble him constantly. It is said in *Dhammapada* that there is no fire like desire.

नत्थी रागसमो अग्गि ।।

Hence nobody can find happiness with a wish fulfilled, rather one can be happy after no wish is cherished. In the *Kathopanishad,* it has been said that a man can attain immortality and realize the real Brahma when all desires are destroyed.

यदा सर्वे प्रमुच्यन्ते कामा येऽस्य हृदि श्रिता: ।
अथ मर्त्योऽमृतो भवत्यत्र ब्रह्मसमश्नुत ।। (2/3/14)

It is observed that man's desires go on increasing as much as his life-span diminishes. There is a story in Marathi which tells us about a rich man. He had a beautiful wife, son and daughter and fame. In spite of all this he desires for more wealth, more name and fame. Once he met a Yakhya whom he prayed to give him more wealth. Immediately the Yakhya gave him money and gold. But he set a condition that his wishes would be fulfilled but he had to press a botton which would be the cause of some one's death. The rich man was in a dilemma. He had to sacrifice his conscience, morality and humanity otherwise he would not be able to satisfy his desire. Finally, he pressed the button and somewhere someone died, but he did not bother about such an inhuman act. Today, human beings have lost their conscience. To achieve one's selfish ends a man can cause mass destruction.

This body is ephemeral, so is wealth. Death is knocking at the door. Sita had to suffer a lot for her greed for the golden deer. That is why one is advised to forsake desires and lead a life based on truthfulness and justice.

The holy book *Subhasitaratnabhandagaram* says :

अनित्यानि शरीराणि विभवो नैव शाश्वतः ।
नित्यं सन्निहितो मृत्युः कर्त्तव्यो धर्मसंग्रहः ।।

The human soul is immortal. Hence it is the duty of man to achieve holiness by practicing righteousness.

Verse – 13

का ते कान्ता धनगतचिन्ता वातुलः किं तव नास्ति नियन्ता ।
त्रिजगति सज्जनसङ्गतिरेका भवति भवार्णवतरणे नौका ।।
भज गोविन्दम् ।। १३ ।।

Meaning – O' mad man with a restless mind! Why are you so much worried about your wife and your wealth? Don't you know that there is one omnipotent entity in this universe which directs everything? In the whole world, holy company is the only ship that is our saviour in this ocean of life and death.

Commentary – Why are you so much worried about your wife and wealth? The world is not meant for enjoying your wife or property. One should not waste one's body and mind for the sake of one's wife and wealth. Worries destroy one's mental power. Once desires capture a man he loses his mental balance. One's personality cannot develop. He feels exhausted in the struggle for existence. He cannot face problems.

Once Basanagupta, a monk in a famous Buddhist monastery was roaming in the city of Pataliputra. He arrived in the house of an extremely beautiful woman, Kosha. When he was accepting alms from her, he was attracted towards her. He forgot about his sacred vows. Crossing the threshold, he entered the inner premises of the house. Kosha thought that perhaps Basantagupta wanted to be treated specially while receiving alms. She directed her attendant to pay proper respect to the monk. But the monk was not satisfied with this. He wanted to meet Kosha in a secret place. When he met her, he expressed his love for her. Kosha was shocked to see such a great monk stooping so low. She did not want to disgrace him. But she agreed to accept his proposal on a condition. She demanded a fixed amount of money from him.

Now the monk went on collecting money from rich people. After getting the required amount of money he came to Kosha. She took all the money and placed it under her feet, then she stamped over it and threw it into the drain. Basantagupta was surprised to see her behave in this manner.

Kosha said, 'You are a holy man. You look pious but I am a prostitute, meant to be enjoyed by all. People feel excited looking at me and also hate me. As I grow oder, my glamour will fade. My body will rot like that money thrown into the drain. Your body will be covered with flowers and mine with worms. Coming in contact with such a body you will be contaminated and degraded.'

After listening to Kosha Basantagupta realized his mistake. He returned to his hermitage feeling disgraced.

Women are not commodities. They should not be treated as sources of pleasure. Such erroneous thoughts enterained by middle aged cause the downfall of human beings. The sex-obsessed and money-minded people are called insane. Such people fall down into the hell only. In order to save oneself from such downfall one has to interact with holy people. The company of holy people is compared with a boat. Such holy company is necessary for one to sail across this world of troubled waters.

A story will make this point clear : One day, the great sage Bashistha went to the sage Viswamitra. He was cordially received. At the time of departure he was offered as a guest half of the effect of his worship. In return, Basistha presented his host with one moment of the result of his holy company. Viswamitra felt that Basistha did not care for him. He must have known the hard worship his host used to do. His worship has a great result. Basistha could guess Viswamitra's inner feelings. He explained that the effect of a good company is far greater than that of worship. Viswamitra was not prepared to accept this. Both started arguing. Finally, they went to Lord Brahma, the creator of this universe for a solution.

Viswamitra was a short-tempered man. He might create problems if the solution was not in his favour. Hence Brahma sent them to Lord Shiva, the God of Destruction. Shiva also did not agree to decide their conflict. They were sent to Lord Vishnu but the Lord said that one of his wives was Laxmi who was always hasty and another was Saraswati who was talkative. With such partners he had become stupefied. Hence He suggested them to go to Vasuki, the Lord of Snakes. Both the sages went to Vasuki who listened to their arguments. Vasuki suggested that he was bearing the load of the world, if someone helped him in bearing the load, he would give them the solution. Viswamitra immediately offered his help. He thought that through penance he had become a great sage. Although he had given half of the result of his worship to Basistha still then with the other half he would be able to bear the load of the earth. But to his dismay, the earth would not move. Vasuki then expected Basistha who had given him the result of only a moment's holy company. Viswamitra was surprised to see the earth lifted from Vasuki's head. He realized the real effect of holy company.

Goswamy Tulsidas explains the effect of holy company. He says that bad company may lead to one's destruction, but with holy company human life becomes fruitful. This is narrated in the Vedas and scriptures. A little bit of dust is lifted to the sky coming in contact with air. The water from the sky does not come to be used by people as it falls on mud. Planets, medicine, water and wind coming in touch of good things become beneficial. If somebody's planet is in good place, it helps the man, if it is in a lesser place, it harms the man. If water is contaminated with poison, it kills a man, but if medicine is added to it, water becomes fruitful and life-saving.

Hence it is rightly said that, when one befriends a bad man, it is certain that one is going to be spoilt. One has to choose one's company with great care.

●

Verse – 14

जटिलो मुण्डी लुण्डितकेशः काषायाम्बरबहुकृतवेशः ।
पश्यन्नपि च न पश्यति मूढः उदरनिमित्तं वहुकृतवेशः ।।
भज गोविन्दम् ।। १४।।

Meaning - Some ascetics wear their hair as head-gear, some move without any hair on their head, some people root out hairs and some others wear yellow clothes – these are really pseudo-monks. They put on various costumes and cheat common men. But they are, in fact, cheating themselves. They can't see reality. They appear in disguise for earning their livelihood.

Commentary - This sloka is composed by Padmapad, the disciple of Shankar. The story of a pseudo-monk has been narrated here. Once the monk was residing in a hermitage built in the upper reaches of the Himalayas. He was spending his time in meditation and the recitation of God's name. He had learnt many ways of performing miracles. Once he desired to leave the snowy Himalayas. He came down and stayed on the plains. People gathered around him when they knew that he was a great sage. They were awed by his wonderful speeches and advice. His beard and his hair shone like gold. People called him 'Swarnakesh'.

One day, while he was walking down the road in a village, a woman ran up to him. She was crying bitterly and was holding her sick child. Earlier her six children had already died. She earnestly requested the sage to save the life of this only child. The sage grew compassionate. He uprooted one of his hairs and gave it to the lady assuring her that her son would be cured soon. Surprisingly the child got well. This news spread far and wide instantly. Thousands of people from distant places rushed to the monk seeking the remedy for their difficulties.

The sage gave one of his hairs to the needy ones. But many people were impatint. They started uprooting hair from his head forcibly. The sage screamed of pain and finally he died. Thus to get name and fame he lost his life. It is not the duty of a god-man to fly in the sky, drink acid, swallow iron nails, walk on fire and stay under the earth for long. Such is the practice of jugglers. The duty of great sages is to get knowledge of the self and propagate the holy message of leading a life devoid of greed, anger, desire and aspirations. The thought of becoming a man of crores and spending a life of luxury is quite hateful as it is responsible for the downfall of society. The so-called holy people are busy in showing off their prowess of dissuading people from committing sinful actions.

One-day, three holy people started meditating. One of them learnt how to walk over the surface of water. Another one learnt how to fly. The third one could live underground for a long time. They earned a lot from the miracles being exhibited to common men. Their name and fame spread in all directions. One day, a genuinely wise man came to meet them, saw their charisma and then told them, 'How many years did you spend in learning these miracles?' All the three said, 'Twelve years'. The wiseman said, 'It is quite unfortunate. This work is done by a mouse, a fly and a fish. You have wasted twelve valuable years of your life in acquiring such skills which a fly, a fish or a rat could easily do. What benefit would you get for human society by acquiring the skills of baser animals? If you want to achieve something as humans then it is best to learn the methods of knowing the self.

Verse – 15

अङ्गं गलितं पलितं मुण्डं दशनविहीनं जातं तुण्डम् ।
वृद्धो यति गृहीत्वा दण्डं तदपि न मुञ्चत्याशापिण्डम् ।।
. भज गोविन्दम् ।। १५।।

Meaning - During old age, the body withers, the organs grow less agite and the skin gets wrinkled. In old age hair grows grey and the teeth fall down. One needs a walking-stick to maintain one's balance. In such condition also men cannot give up their desires.

Commentary – In *Vairagya Shatakam*, Bhartrihari has commented on old age :

गात्रं संकुञ्चितं गतिर्विगलिता भ्रष्टा च दन्तावली
दृष्टिर्नश्यति वर्धते वधिरता वक्त्रं च लालायते ।
वाक्यं नाद्रियते च बान्धवजनो भार्या न शुश्रूषते
हा कष्टं पुरुषस्य जीर्णवयसः पुत्रोऽप्यमित्रायते ।

Memory fades, relatives don't listen to you,
Wives don't take care of you, children behave like strangers.
One has no strength to walk,
Sans teeth, sans vision,
This old age becomes very painful.

The state of old age is one of the reasons which influenced prince Siddharth to forsake his throne. In spite of losing all physical powers and advancing towards death one cannot give up one's desires. This is real attachment. This pushes a man into an abysmal depth of misery. Desires accumulate alongwith man's advancing years. All his desires and aspirations are destroyed with his death only.

One day, sage Narad met Yama, the Lord of Death. Narad asked, Sir, what is the cause of the strange fact that people do not leave their desires in spite of suffering a lot from diseases, hunger and sorrows? The Lord of Death asked him to accompany him invisibly. It was hot noon. They saw an old woman of eighty walking to the market carrying a basket-ful watermelons. She took rest in the street under a tree. Narad in disguise went to her and asked, 'Grandma, how are you?'

The old woman said, 'See how the Lord of Death, so cruel, is not taking my life. How much I am suffering ! He must be having a poor memory.'

Narad looked at the Lord. He smiled, did not tell him anything. They saw the old woman trying to lift the pot of watermelons on to her head.

Narad wanted to know the reaction of Lord of Death. The Lord appeared before the old woman. She got shocked looking at the strangers. She asked, 'Who are you?' Narad replied, 'I am Narad and He is the Lord of Death. Moments ago you were calling him. Now see, Lord of Death has appeared to relieve you of your pains.'

The old woman said, 'What? Why should I die ? I have told to my grandson that I am getting sweets for him after selling watermelons. My grand-daughter has been engaged recently. She will marry soon. The eldest daughter-in-law will deliver a child.'

Narad said, 'O.K. don't worry. Because you wanted to meet the Lord of Death, I called him. Now you go on troubling yourself as much as you live.'

The old woman said, 'Did I desire to die sincerely? Because I could not lift the pot of watermelon, I complained. Don't the Gods ever take things lightly and jokingly ?'

Both Narad and Lord of Death laughed and helped her lift the load.

Swami Shivananda narrates another interesting story. There was an old man named Bithal living at the foot of the Bindhya mountain. He owned nothing except the cottage where he was taking shelter. Once he got news that a sage had come there.

He had miraculous powers. The old man approached him and requested for wealth. The holy man felt compassion for him. He gave him a magic mat and said, 'Whenever you sit on this and wish for something, you will get it instantly.'

The old man thanked the holy man and came back home. He took bath and then sat on the mat. He felt hungry. He wanted to have delicious food. Immediately tasty food arrived. Then he wanted a comfortable bed. He got it. The bed was fit for a palace. Hence Bithal wanted a palace. Instantly there was a huge palace in place of the small hut. Then he thought there must be jewels in such big house. Immediately the house was filled with jewellery. The old man desired for servants. Soon he found many attendants standing before him with folded hands. Bithal was so overjoyed. He was mentally troubled when he worried about what would happen to all this luxury if there was an earthquake! Suddenly there was an earthquake and the whole structure fell down and turned to pieces. Along with the attendants the old man succumbed to death. With death only his desires came to an end.

There is another instructive story. One day, a sage named Hayagrib met the saintly king Janaka. Then he went to Narad. He said that Janaka is too attached to worldly matters. Why are you praising him so much? If Janaka would meditate in the forest, leaving behind all his attachments he would get liberation.

Narad said, 'O sage, please stay with King Janaka for some days. Then you can understand him. Hayagriba agreed and stayed in Janak's palace as his guest. He was given a special room. All that he possessed was a metal jug and a piece of cloth to be worn round the waist.

One day, the sage was sitting in the court with Janak. Matters of state were discussed. Suddenly there was fire in the palace. People were worried, running and shouting. Hayagrib ran to his room. He collected his belongings and then came back to the conference hall. He was surprised to see Janak still engaged in his official works. There was no trace of anxiety in his face. Hayagrib was surprised.

Just at this time Narad arrived there. He said to the sage, 'You are living in a forest. You have left everything worldly. But you could not bear the loss of such insignificant things like a pot and a piece of cloth. You ran to save your belongings but see, Janak who is still sitting here in spite of the destruction of the palace building. What is the use of forsaking everything and living in the forest?'

The sage felt humbled. He now praised Janak. Narad had actually created the fire. It was an illusion. With his blessings the lustre of the palace was restored.

Janak explained the cause of his happiness –

सुसुखं बत जीवामि यस्य मे नास्ति काञ्चन ।

मिथिलायां प्रदीप्तायां न मे दह्यति किञ्चन । (Valmiki Ramayan)

'I have nothing of my own. Hence I am happy. I don't bother even if the entire kingdom of Mithila gets burnt.'

Sarbapalli Radhakrishnan, the great philosopher who was the President of India, once said, 'Desire is never satisfied by enjoyment of the objects of desire; it grows more and more as does the fire to which fuel is added.'

Actually, material pleasures are like scabies. If one treats it temporarily one is satiated but the main disease gets aggravated. Once a man derives pleasure from treating the disease, he gets more and more entangled in it. It leads to disillusionment.

Those who are slaves of sensual pleasures become slaves of all. On the other hand those who have conquered desires, the whole world comes under their control.

Verse – 16

अग्रे वह्निः पृष्ठे भानुः रात्रौ चिवुकसमर्पितजानुः ।
करतलभिक्षस्तरुतलवासस्तदपि न मुञ्चत्याशापाशम् ।।
भज गोविन्दम् ।। १६ ।।

Meaning – The ascetic sits near a fire or under the sun in order to get relieved from cold. Due to lack of warm dresses he sleeps at night keeping his head between his legs. He takes rest under a tree after begging for alms with folded hands. Still then he cannot free himself from the bondage of desire.

Commentary – In the previous sloka it has been discussed how a dying man cannot leave his desires. The sage also lives under the same condition. He has abdicated all worldly luxuries. He has no home, no food nor any dress. Sun rays and fire only warm him in the cold season. He cannot sleep well for cold. He is underfed and knows not whether he would be given alms the next day. Although he has forsaken the essential things of life still he has not cut himself off from hopes and desires. If one withdraws from worldly pleasures one will remain a psudo-monk unless he frees himself from attachments.

Such a life of hypocrisy is very much like a demon's prayer. In order to give up desire and greed one has to strengthen one's mind.

There is a story about this. Once a king went on a hunting expedition. Suddenly he saw a wild tiger with three cubs. He ran for life. By chance he fell into a dark and deep well. He held the branch of a tree that grew inside the well. The tiger was waiting above. The small tree was weak enough to bear his load. Unfortunately a crocodile was looking at him from inside the water. If the branch breaks, he would fall straight into the crocodile's mouth. There were still more danger. There was a poisonous snake in the branch that the king was holding. It was looking at the king and waiting for a chance to bite him. It seems as if the messengers of the Lord of Death had surrounded him from all sides. There was no chance to save himself from death. In such a critical moment drops of honey fell from the beehive. The entire beehive had been poisoned as a poisonous insect had left poison in it. Who could know it? The king knew that death was inevitable. There was no chance of survival. Still he could not control his greed. He bent down to taste that drop of honey. Thus he lost his life.

The Odia poet, Radhanath Ray speaks of the ignorance of men, which is narrated in the following story : A certain beggar was admitted in a hospital. He could not recover in spite of his doctors' care. Death approached him. Getting this news a clergy came to him to pray for his soul. He requested him to pray to God. The patient could lift one of his hands only. The other hand was stiff. The clergy asked him to fold his hands. The patient said in a low voice, 'I won't open the other palm!' Then he died. His fist was opened to the surprise of all. It contained some dirty currency notes.

The beggar knows that he is going to die still he cannot get rid of his attachment to money. This is called greed and attachment. This happens to every body. Man nurses his desires until his very end. The world is ephemeral and full of suffering. Desires make people suffer. When a man cannot fulfill his desires and greed for more he takes recourse to foul means.

Hopes have no end. They grow luxuriantly. This world is like a pitcher. Our family is smaller than the mouth of the pitcher. Our desires are like food. We are busy in collecting this food from this worldly pitcher. If we forsake our desires then only we can live peacefully. Human desires are also compared to a forest. Each desire is a tree. The forest of desires is a terrible place. If we cut a tree from a forest nothing happens to it. The whole forest is to be cleared. Then only one can achieve one's goal. This is also emphasised in *Dhammapada,*

वनं छिन्दथ मा रुक्खं वनतो जायती भयम् ।
छेत्वा वनं च वनथं च निव्वना होथ भिक्खवे ।।

The Odia poet, Vyasakabi Fakirmohan has said the following :

The wise, the saint, the brave and the poet
No one has ever been free from greed.

Verse – 17

कुरुते गङ्गासागरगमनं व्रतपरिपालनमथवा दानम् ।
ज्ञानविहीनः सर्वमतेन भजति न मुक्तिं जन्मशतेन ।।
भज गोविन्दम् ।। १७।।

Meaning – One can be a pilgrim, visit Gangasagar and many holy places. One can fast, can give gifts, can do rituals. But unless one acquires spiritual knowledge about what is Truth, one cannot attain salvation through such external activities even in hundred lives.

Commentary – One may go to Kashi, Badrinath, Puri, Dwarika and Rameswar on pilgrimage, worship gods and goddesses, donate liberally, thus gets inclined towards spirituality but this is not enough to attain divinity. Real wisdom does not come out of studies. One may be wise, deliver sermons, but one may not be free from worldly desires, may not acquire spiritual wisdom. With such external show one can be established and recognised as a great knowledgeable man, but with this one's soul cannot be liberated. In the *Bhagabad Gita* it is written,

आत्मसंभाविताः स्तब्धाः धनमानमदान्विताः ।
यजन्ते नामयज्ञैस्ते दम्भेनाविधिपुर्वकम् ।। (16 / 17)

It means that the deceiptful man, the insolent, the proud and the rich make a show of donating and worshiping. They build temples to achieve name. It is the same as drinking alcohol at night and going to a temple in the morning.

There is a beautiful story in Rome. One day, the Emperor of Rome, Madrian adked Josua, the Jewish preacher, to show him God. The preacher said that it was impossible to show God. The King did not allow him to leave. He got angry with him and said, 'You have to show me God.' The preacher found himself at his wit's end. One day he called the King at mid-day and suggested to look up to the Sun. It was very difficult for the King to look at the dazzling mid-day sun. The king finally said, I can't do this.'

The preacher explained to the King that, not only one sun, but innumerable planets, stars, gods and goddess are engaged in the service of God. If you can't bear to look at one sun, how can you see the conglomeration of suns. The king realized his mistake. Unless one's mind is drawn towards divinity one can never see God.

One of Ramkrishna's sermons has been delivered here. One night two friends started a journey to enjoy themselves at night. On the street they saw a religious conference going on. Many wise men were busy discussing religious matters. One of these friends wanted to listen to the recitation of God's name. The other one went to a prostitute's house to enjoy himself. The first one listened to this serious religious discouses. After some time he thought that he was deprived of worldly enjoyments. The other friend repented for his misdeed. He thought that he had committed a big mistake by leaving the holy place of religious discourse. Thus the first one is mentally engaged in mean thoughts even while sitting in a spiritual meeting whereas the other one was engrossed in divine thoughts in spite of engaging in bodily pleasures.

In the *'Gita'* it is said,

कर्मेन्द्रियाणि संयम्य य आस्ते मनसा स्मरन् ।
इन्द्रियार्थान् विमूढात्मा मिथ्याचारः सः उच्यते ।। (3 / 6)

It means that a man while forcibly exercising control over his five sensory organs – mouth, hands, feet, ears & eyes thinks of worldly enjoyments. So he deceives himself. One cannot be liberated through a semblance of an ascetic life.

●

Verse – 18

सुरमन्दिरतरुमूलनिवासः शय्या भूतलमजिनं वासः ।
सर्वपरिग्रहभोगत्यागः कस्य सुखं न करोति विरागः ।।
भज गोविन्दम् ।। १८।।

Meaning – Sitting in the temple or under the tree, sleeping in the floor, wearing deer skin, giving up all the enjoyable things – all this produces celestial pleasure attained with a sense of detachment. Renunciation gives more pleasure than enjoyment. In *Vairagya Satakam* it is said :

मेही रम्या शय्या विपुलमुपधानं भुजलता
वितानं चाकाशं व्यजनमनुकूलोऽयमनिलः ।
स्फुरद्दीपश्चन्द्रो विरतिवनितासङ्गमुदितः
सुखं शान्तः शेते मुनिरतनुभूतिर्नृप इव ।।

Commentary – What Bhartrihari had said in Bairagya Sataka, in the same way F.T.Cheng has said, 'With only coarse rice as meal and only plain water as drink, and only my arm as pillow, I still find joy in the midst of these conditions. Wealth and honour compared with righteousness are to me like the passing cloud.'

The last sloka describes a false saint. In this sloka it is shown how a real yogi or renouncer gets immense pleasure from nature.

Nobody is happy in this world. A king is anxious to be an emperor. A man of lakhs desires to be a man of crores. A beautiful girl wants to be a world beauty. Nobody tolerates another's glory. Envy and malice make him unhappy. Happiness or peace is a mental condition. It is not a commercial matter that can be attained through exchange.

In the *Panchatantra* there is a wonderful story about the bharanda birds, which suffered from envy. This bird lived by a sea. It had two heads. Once, while wandering on the beach, the bird found a nice ripe fruit. While eating one of its heads said to the other that the fruit tasted wonderful, as if it was a sweet fruit sent by gods. The other head said, 'Please give me the fruit. I want to taste it.' The first head said, 'See, we both have one stomach. Hence whatever I take you have also taken.' The second head felt bad. He waited for the time when he would be able to take revenge.

One day, a poisonous fruit lay on the sea beach. The second head wanted to taste it. The first head tried to stop him but he would not listen. He said, 'O foolish one, I want to take revenge on you, I will take it.' Saying this he took the fruit and the bird died.

Another story goes like this : Once upon a time there was a king who had no wants. He had everything that one desires – beautiful queens, immense wealth, ministers, courtiers, soldiers and servants. In spite of all this he was not happy. He was always worried.

He called his ministers and faithful servants and told them about this. He begged for their advice. Once servant made bold to suggest, 'Sir, music gives pleasure. You listen to music from morning to evening'. The king did not believe that music could give him happiness. Another one suggested, 'Sir, you enjoy the beauty of nature. The green earth, the star-studded sky and the moonlit night – all this can change your mind. I am sure, you will find peace and pleasure'. The king was not satisfied. He shouted loudly and ran towards the storeroom. The store-keeper said humbly,

'Sir, I am suggesting to you a small thing. You call a happy man and wear his shirt. I am sure you will attain happiness.'

The king agreed. Immediately he called the soldiers and commanded, 'Try to find the happiest man in our kingdom and bring him here.' The soldiers scoured the kingdom but could not find a happy man. They were returning disappointed, when suddenly they saw a monk singing divine songs sitting under a tree. His face was shining. They asked him, 'Sir who is the happiest man?' He said, 'Myself'. The soldiers took the monk to the king. The monk was laughing and uttering words in praise of God. The king came to him, saluted him and then asked him to give him his shirt, so that he would live happily like him.

Alas ! There was no shirt on the monk's body. The king was surprised to know that the happiest man in the world has no shirt. At last he realized the truth. He changed the style of his living. He learnt that only a life of detachment can bring peace and happiness.

The Philosopher and former President of India Radhakrishnan had said, 'We should reduce our wants and be prepared to suffer in the interest of truth. Austerity, chastity, solitude and silence are the ways to attain self-control.'

In the *Vairagya Shatakam* it has been explained –

वयमिह परितुष्टा वल्कलैस्त्वं दुकूलैः

समझव परितोषो निर्विशेषविशेषः ।
स तु भवतु दरिद्रो यस्य तृष्णा विशाला
मनसि च परितुष्टे कोऽर्थवान् को दरिद्रः ।।

It means that a man however wealthy cannot be happy if he is poor mentally, whereas one who remains always contented is really a happy one.

These are the significant traits of a detached man. The poet Bhartruhari has compared a king with a saint. A saint is always the best. He always waits for that good day when he can attain detachment.

A real monk removes all desires from his mind. In the Sankhya Yoga Chapter, Lord Krishna had said,

प्रजहाति यदा कामान् सर्वान् पार्थ मनोगतान् ।
आत्मन्येवात्मना तुष्टः स्थितप्रज्ञस्तदोच्यते ।। (2/55)

Krishna says – O Arjun, when a man relinquishes all his sensual desires and gets mental satisfaction, he is called 'sthitaprangyan' – a liberated soul.

As heat is born of fire, so also happiness is derived from the soul. The soul is full of happiness. Without this knowledge the ignorant people search for pleasure from external things. That is desire. When one's desires go away from one's mind one gets divine pleasure. Those wise people who are engrossed in the pleasure of the soul, they are really liberated souls. The materialists argue that one cannot be successful in ones works if there is no desire, but such a view is wrong. When one works with a sense of detachment, one's efficiency increases.

Ego is created out of ignorance. All desires, attachment and infatuation are created out of ego. When divinity dawns discarding ego, ignorance disappears like mist. Once ego is destroyed, the heart becomes clean and sacred. It becomes easy to realize the self and a man can attain liberation. He attains the state of 'sthitapragyan'.

Verse – 19

योगरतो वा भोगरतो वा सङ्गरतो वा सङ्गविहीनः ।
यस्य ब्रह्मणि रमते चितं नन्दति नन्दति नन्दत्येव ।।
भज गोविन्दम् ।। १९ ।।

Meaning – One whose mind is settled in Brahma, the Supreme Soul, will enjoy real pleasure whether he is engaged in yogic exercises or in luxuries, or is part of a crowd or lives alone.

Analysis – In the *Bhagabad Gita,* it is said –

मन्मना भव मद्भक्तो मद्याजी मां नमस्कुरु ।
मामेवैषसि युक्त्वैवमात्मानं मत्परायणः ।। (9 / 34)

Commentary - Attach your mind to me all the time. I am all pervasive, all powerful and all knowledgeable. A total surrender is essential. One's worship must be free from expectations. Then only can you attain divinity. God had rescued the deer in the forest. He had saved the elephant from the jaws of a crocodile. He had torn the heart of Hiranyakashpu emerging from a pillar. He had also saved Draupadi from disgrace. God listens to one who makes complete surrender to Him unencumbered by ego.

Once a disciple asked a sage, 'O Lord, you say that God is omniscient, omnipresent and omnipotent. But I cannot realize His existence. I cannot ask you thinking that you may laugh at me and tell me that I am an atheist.' The sage replied, 'Son, I am pleased with your question. If you want to realize divinity, come with me.' Both of them entered a pond. Suddenly the saint pressed the disciple's head into water. He felt breathless. After struggling hard he pushed the sage and came out of water. He shouted at the sage, 'Have you brought me here to kill me?'

The sage calmly said, 'Son, what were you thinking when you were under water?'

The man said, 'Sir, my only thought was how to come out of water and take breath. If needed, I would have drowned you under the water.'

The sage said, 'My dear son, now realize that Without confidence and concentration it is impossible to reach the infinity.'

Here, one incident about Swami Vivekananda is worth recounting : When he was in America, some students were learning shooting. The covers of three eggs were tied to a thread and were floating in a spring. Students were aiming at them; but could not be successful in shooting. Vivekananda laughed. The boys felt offended as a foreigner was laughing at their failure. They gave the gun to him. Vivekananda held the gun for the first time in his life. He aimed at the eggs and hit them. The boys were astonished. They asked, 'How is it that you aimed so perfectly although it was the first time you held a gun?' Swamiji smiled and said, 'Determination and concentration is the only clue for success.'

In spite of being a householder, one can attain immortality performing our tasks with detachment. One nice example may be cited here. There was a poor woman. She was always busy with her household works. When she making flattened rice she was also feeding her baby. If any customer came, she bargained with them. Amidst all these works she had fixed her attention on her hands so that they won't get crushed in the machine. This is called concentration. There is a story of another woman who used to walk on a bamboo while engaging in frolic but all the time her mind was fixed on her feet so that she won't fall down. In the same manner a householder can perform all his worldly duties settling his mind on God.

The life of the king and sage Janaka is worth citing here. Once the sage Kamapala was explaining to his disciple how the mind is the root cause of attachment. It is not correct to say that one can attain liberation relinquishing worldly pleasures. A man can recognize God keeping one's mind holy like Janaka who was leading a householder's life. Listening to this the disciple went to the palace of the king Janaka. He saw the king meditating. His wife was sitting on his left thigh. The disciple got confused. He said that he had never seen such a shameless man. He did not deserve praise.

The sage Kamapala along with his disciple arrived at the King's palace. He placed a burning charcoal in his palm. His hand was burnt. There was a foul smell. Still his mind was not troubled. He was still deep in meditation. His face was looking brilliant as he was engrossed in divinity. He could not feel what was happening to his body. He was undisturbed. The bonds of the world could not confine him. The disciple repented realizing his mistake. After sometime the king got up. He smiled at the sage and his disciple. He greeted them cordially. Hence it is understood that while leading a domestic life dutifully a householder if he prays to God, He will appear to him. There is no doubt about it.

Verse – 20

भगवद्गीता किञ्चिदधीता गङ्गाजललवकणिका पीता ।
सकृदपि येन मुरारिसमर्चा क्रियते तस्य यमेन न चर्चा ।।
भज गोविन्दम् ।। २० ।।

Meaning – One who reads the Gita regularly, takes the water of the Ganges, prays to God even for some time, the Lord of Death cannot harm him. He is bound to be liberated.

Commentary – Reading the Gita, taking Ganges water and praying to God are easy courses of the spiritual programme. Each religion has its scriptures. The Christians have the *Bible,* the Mohammodans have the *Koran,* the Sikhs have the *Grantha Sahib,* and the Persians have the *Zenda vesta.* Likewise the Hindu religion's central ideas are found in the *Srimad Bhagabat Gita.* Why is *Gita* so important? Because whatever problems arise in worldly struggles, the Gita provides solutions. Gandhiji found his principle of non-violence from the *Gita.* Valuable advice is given in the *Gita* about a life of detachment.

सर्वोपनिषदो गावो दोग्धा गोपालनन्दनः ।
पार्थो वत्सः सुधीर्भोक्ता दुग्धं गीतामृतं महत् ।। (Gita Dhyanam)

It means the *Upanishad* is mother cow. The *Gita* is her milk. Lord Krishna milks the cow and gives it to Arjun. Again, it is said that whoever reads the *Gita* amidst all his household works gets liberated after his demise.

गीतार्थं ध्यायते नित्यं कृत्वा कर्माणि भूरिशः ।
जीवन्मुक्तः स विज्ञेयो देहान्ते परमं पदम् ।। (Gita Mahatmyam)

The water of Ganges is considered holy by the Hindus. The King Bhagirath had brought the stream of the river Ganges from heaven down to the earth to save his forefathers. The river had come out of the nail of Lord Krishna and then entered Lord Shiva's hair knot. That is why it is holy. The river passed the plain land starting from the Himalaya. Many places of pilgrimage are situated at the side of the holy river. The Hindus believe that one spoonful of Ganges river water in the mouth of a dying man liberates him. Taking a dip in the river also purifies man. The Ganges is thus a symbol of the Hindu religion and culture. Some modern people speak of the devotion to Ganga as superstition. Should we dismiss our national flag as a piece of cloth in three different colours? It is a symbol of our national integrity. It is our pride. Likewise the Ganges is holy to every Hindu.

About recitation of God's name one can take the example of the thief Ratnakar who chanted Lord Ram's name and turned into a great sage, Valmiki. Ajamil, a Brahmin, recited the name of Lord Vishnu and after his death his soul was carried to heaven.

There is a nice story about the significance of chanting God's name. A wise man lived beside a river. A milkmaid was living on the other side of the river. The wise man was worshipping God. One day the milkmaid was late. The wise man was waiting for milk. As soon as the milkmaid arrived, he scolded her severely. She said, 'Sir, the river was in spate. It is still raining heavily. The boatman was not there. How could I come?' The wise man said, 'Why did not you chant the name of Ram? People chant this name and cross the river.'

The next morning the milkmaid came early. The wise man asked. 'Did the boatman come early today?' The milkmaid said, 'You gave me the trick. So I uttered Ram's name and walked across the river.'

The wise man was surprised to hear this. He had doubts. He went to the river following her. She chanted the name of Lord Ram and crossed the river. The wise man started chanting Ram's name. He pulled up his dress so that he would not get drenched. The milkmaid shouted, 'Sir, if you are chanting Ram's name, you should not worry about your clothes. You have no faith in God. How can you cross the river of the world.'

The wise man realized his mistake. He saluted the woman's simple faith and then returned home.

Hence it is proved that not with arguments but with faith only can one attain divinity.

Verse – 21

पुनरपि जननं पुनरपि मरणं पुनरपि जननीजठरे शयनम् ।
इह संसारे खलु दुस्तारे कृपयाऽपारे पाहि मुरारे ! ।।
भज गोविन्दम् ।। २१ ।।

Meaning – All creatures take birth, grow, then die. After death he comes to his mother's womb again. This cycle of birth, death and birth makes his life painful. Without divine grace liberation from this life and death cycle is not possible. O'God, please save me through your grace from such worldly suffering !

Commentary – In the *Bhagabad* Gita it is said –

जातस्य हि ध्रुवो मृत्यु:र्ध्रुवं जन्म मृतस्य च ।
तस्मादपरिहार्येऽर्थे न त्वं शेचितुमर्हसि ।। (2/27)

Whoever takes birth is sure to die and after death one is reborn. This life and death cycle is inevitable. One should not feel sad about this.

Again it is said :

न त्वेवाहं जातु नासं न त्वं नेमे जनाधिपाः ।
न चैव न भविष्यामः सर्वे वयमतः परम् ।। (2/12)

It is not truth that there was a time when I was not there, you were not there and all these kings were not there. It is not true that none of us will be there in future.

It is further said -

देहिनोऽस्मिन् यथा देहे कौमारं यौवनं जरा ।
तथा देहान्तरप्राप्तिर्धीरस्तत्र न मूह्यति ।। (2/13)

Whoever possesses a body has to pass through different stages. He has to pass through childhood, youth, adulthood and old age at the proper time and then leave his body. He will acquire a new body as one gives up one's torn cloth and needs a new one. As he never regrets leaving his tattered clothes, so also he should not feel sad when he has to leave his decayed body, which would be no more useful for him.

As Lord Krishna explained to Arjun in the *Gita* -

अव्यत्कादीनि भूतानि व्यत्कमध्यानि भारत !।
अव्यत्कनिधनान्येव तत्र का परिवेदना ।। (2/28)

It means that all creatures were unknown before birth and after birth they will remain so. Only during the middle stage they appear to be expressive. Why should then one be worried about this?

In order to get relief from such a poisonous cycle, a man has to leave worldly activities. He has to be engaged in useful work. A worm prepares a net while growing up. But gradually it gets entangled in the net itself. In such a confined state it changes into a butterfly. After becoming a butterfly, it flies from one flower to another. It has already forgotten what it was at the beginning. Preparing a net and getting out of it are the two worthy tasks of the insect. Human life goes through similar experiences of getting birth and dying again like the butterfly. If he can renounce all his hopes and desires then only he can be liberated to join divinity. Removing ego from one's mind and surrendering oneself completely to God one can attain divine grace. One cannot escape death becoming afraid of it. There is a sloka in the *Panchatantra*, which says:

मृत्योर्विभेषि किं मूढ़ ! भीतमुञ्झति किं यमः ।
अजातं नैव गृह्णाति कुरु त्वं जन्मजन्मनि ।।

(Mitraveda 152)

Why are you afraid of death? Can ever death spare a coward ? The Lord of Death never touches a man, who is unborn. Hence try not to take birth again.

In the *Mahabharat* there is a pathetic scene describing the plight of Droupadi when Dushasan was pulling her cloth, make her stand naked. Elderly person like Bhishma, Drona, Kripacharya, Veedur sat in court lowering their gaze. Droupadi cried in despair. She felt helpless as her five husbands kept quiet. She prayed to Lord Krishna raising one of her hands. She used the other hand to hold fast to her cloth. She thought that Lord Vishnu had heard the prayers of the elephant and the deer in distress, but why was He so cruel to her? He had always helped the Pandabas and why was he now not listening to her prayers? When she found that as he could not save her dignity from the ruthless Dushashan, she lost faith in her own strength, then she prayed to God with folded hands to rescue her from her disgrace. Immediately divine grace was showered on her and a lot of clothes came down to cover her body. Dushashan got tired of pulling her clothes. The whole audience was stunned. Everybody should learn from this instance that one cannot gain divine grace through meditation, chanting songs or prayers only; one has to completely surrender oneself before God. Hence in the *Gita*, Lord Krishna strongly advocates complete surrender -

सर्वधर्मान् परित्यज्य मामेकं शरणं व्रज ।
अहं त्वां सर्वपापेभ्यो मोक्षयिष्यामि मा शुच ।। (18 / 66)

God asks Arjun to forsake all religions and submit to Him. He can liberate His devotees from all kinds of evil deeds. There is nothing to worry about. These are His words. God has killed two demons – Mura and Daruna, hence he is called Murari. Mura and Daruna are symbol of desire and aspiration. Hence one is advised to restrain oneself and give up one's desires. Then only can one attain liberation from this mundane world.

Verse – 22

रथ्याचर्पटविरचितकन्थः पुण्यापुण्यविवर्जितपन्थः ।
योगी योगनियोजितचितो रमते बालोन्मत्तवदेव ।।
भज गोविन्दम् ।। २२ ।।

Meaning – Clad in rags picked from the street a yogi walks on his way without worrying about good or evil. He gets lost in meditation. The yogi in such condition behaves like an innocent child or an insane person.

Commentary – Bhartrihari has explained such a condition in *Vairagya Shatakam*. Once a man attains eternal wisdom, his ego vanishes. He pays no attention to his body. Sometimes he appears like a simple child and at other times he behaves like an insane man. A child's mind is full of love and affection. There is no trace of impurity. Children easily forget what they had done some time ago. They cannot think ill of anybody. The poetess Kuntala Kumari draws a beautiful picture of a child.

How beautiful O child!
You have no worry!
Your new life is
Full of nectar.
You have no greed, no anger.
No malice nor any ambition.
You have no sense of differentiation
You have not nurtured a selfish worm.

In fact, there is much similarity between a saint and a child. A saint does not distinguish between the great and the small. He shows no anger, greed and ego. Hence he never fills hopeless. He has no need to repent for the past nor has any future plans. He never gets lost in happiness nor in sorrow. Hence it is rightly said in the *Gita* :

दुःखेष्वनुद्विग्नमनाः सुखेषु विगतस्पृहः ।
वीतरागभयक्रोधः स्थितधीर्मुनिरुच्यते ।। (2 / 56)

One, who is not perturbed by sorrows nor gets overwhelmed by pleasure feels no anger, fear nor greed, is really a blessed soul. He surrenders himself to God without paying heed to prayers and recitations of the virtues of divinity. He does not nourish any worldly aspirations. The only thought that engrosses him is that he belongs to God and God belongs to him. He never thinks about the pros and cons of his worldly life, whether God is the creator, master and destroyer of this world.

There is a story about Hanuman, the staunch devotee of Sri Ram-

One day, Ram, Sita and Hanuman were sitting under a tree. The leaves of a creeper covered the tree. The beauty of the tree was enhanced by the flowers and leaves of the creeper. Sri Ram said to Hanuman, 'Look at this creeper and watch how it has increased the beauty of the tree. This tree looks more beautiful than the others for this creeper only. For this creeper only so many birds are taking rest in the tree. Let us thank the creeper.'

Sita said, 'You must have noticed how the creeper with its leaves, scented flowers and sweet fruits depends on the tree. All this is possible only for the tree. The tree is in fact responsible for the beauty of the creeper. Hence the tree deserves praise. Without the tree how can the creeper live?' She asked Hanuman to say whether the tree is more glorious than the creeper.

Hanuman analysed the comments made by Sri Ram and Sita on the tree and the creeper. He said, O' God, I think differently from both of you. Both the tree and the creeper offer shade giving rest to all. I like to take shelter in both as I need to take rest at the feet of both of you. Please satisfy my desire.

The real saints are above evil and good. They are not afraid of anybody. They don't bother aout diseases, old age, death, disgrace, justice and injustice because they lead a life of detachment. They have no desire for any kind of mundane possessions.

Bhartrihari in his *Vairagya Shatakam* describes this state attained by saintly persons.

भोगो रोगभयं कुले च्युतिभयं वत्त नृपालाद्भयं
माने दैन्यभयं बले रिपुभयं रूपे जराया भयम् ।
रास्वे वादभयं गुणे खलभयं काये कृतान्ताद्भयं
सर्वं वस्तु मयान्वितं मुवि नृणां वैराग्यमेवाभयम् ।।

All kinds of work involve risk. Sensuous enjoyment leads to physical ailments. There is fear of disgrace and of enemies when one grows physically strong. There are fears of old age and of poverty also. If one becomes wise, one fears scriptures in conflict with each other. A talented person is afraid of ill-motivated persons. Above all, this, the physical being of a man, is full of fear of death. Only detachment begets no fear.

There are different kinds of insane people. Some are mad after wealth, some are crazy for knowledge. Some pursue love and some others, devotion. Those who are detached love only God. Great devotees like Chaitanya and Ramkrishna belong to this category. The monks have no needs. They rest under a tree. They need no clothes nor food. Their only possession is a mat and a pot. Now-a-days people have different approaches to life. They want to lead a luxurious life without doing any labour. Today, nobody cherishes sacrifice as an ideal. Everybody hankers for enjoyment. In such a time of complications only God is our saviour.

●

Verse – 23

कस्त्वं कोऽहं कुत: आयात: का मे जननी को मे तात: ।
इति परिभावय सर्वमसारं विश्वं त्यक्त्वा स्वप्नविचारम् ।।
भज गोविन्दम् ।। २३ ।।

Meaning – Who are you? Who am I? Where from did I come to this world? Who is my mother? Who is my Father?

Considering all these questions one can find everything in this life worthless. Everything is like an illusion and imaginary.

Commentary – Man dreams in his sleep at night. Sometimes dreams turn terrifying and painful. When one wakes up the dream vanishes and one gets relieved from one's tension. Acharya Shankar has compared life with a dream. All our feelings and experiences are like things we find in our dreams. That is why I must know who I am. Where did I come from? What would happen to me after death? Instead of trying to discover the secret of life we are engaged in illusionary matters. The ego hurts us.

We take our parents, brothers and sisters and kith and kin as dear ones. For such attachments very often we do unjust deeds. Deep thought would tell us that none of them is related to the soul. They would never befriend us when we face death. I have no knowledge about my previous lives. In the last birth I had parents and relatives. Can we ever think of each other? The branches of a tree while floating in a river in flood, join together for some time and again they get separated in the surging tide. Likewise, we also get connected in one life and get disconnected after death. Hence our relationships should be based on duty only.

The *Mahabharat* describes how Arjun threw away his bow and promised not to fight any more after he saw his son Abhimanyu was killed by the Kourabas through deceit. Lord Krishna tried to pacify him. He advised Arjun to understand how death is the only truth and physical existence must come to an end. Nobody is really related to us. But Arjun was not convinced. Then Lord Krishna offered to show him Abhimanyu. He said, 'After you see your son, you will find out if you can get him back.'

Krishna guided Arjun beyond a hill. There was neither the earth nor the sun. They had to cross the Sudarshan wheel. They noticed there was another wheel moving parallel to the Sudarshan wheel. Many children were playing over the spokes of this wheel. All are handsome. Srikrishna asked Arjun to recognize his own son. When Arjun saw his son and called him affectionately the boy could not recognize him. He ran away. When Arjun saw him again, he requested to come back to the world with him. He said that, Uttara, his mother was crying, not taking any food. The boy replied, 'You say you are my father, but do you know how many times you were my son in our last births? Hence go back to the earth. As long as there is the body, relationships are of any consequence. Hence please do not disturb me.'

Saying this Abhimanyu ran away. Arjun's sense of attachment was shattered.

One day, sage Astabakra arrived at the court of the King Janaka. The king said, 'If you can give a fitting answer to my question I will consider you a true scholar.' Astabakra said politely, 'O King, there are innumerable questions in this world which are not solved. That is why this world brought into being by the creator lies beyond human knowledge. It will be insolent on my part to solve your problem.' Now Janak realised that Astabakra was not ordinary sage. He told him, 'I saw in a dream that I am begging alms. Suddenly, two bulls came and started fighting each other. In their fight my bowl fell down and was broken. My stomach was empty. My eyes were full of tears. Just at that moment I woke up. I found myself sleeping on a comfortable bed. I became aware of reality. I found myself not a beggar, but a king.' So the king asked the sage what was real : his dream or his waking state ? Astabakra smiled and said, 'O'Lord, both are the same.' Janaka was overwhelmed as he found the answer so simple and easy.

Swetaketu, Astabakra's friend was there. He was surprised. He could not understand what the sage said. Hence Astabakra explained to him that the luxuries in the palace as well as the grief of the hungry beggar who sheds tears are both dreams. Hence both are the same. Whatever we see in dream while we sleep is an illusion and what we see fully awake is also an illusion. The world, like a dream, is useless and temporary.

Once Ramkrishna Paramhansha gave a nice example. There was a wood-cutter. One day he saw in a dream that he was a king. His treasury was full of wealth. He had a beautiful wife and seven children. All were quite efficient. As his wife called him while he was in a wonderful dream-world, his joys vanished immediately. He was shocked to find that all his seven sons soon disappeared.

Let us narrate another incident. A certain needy man was leading a miserable life. His only son was ill. His wife blamed him. One day the son expired. All were mourning. The man left the house to earn something. After a long period, when he returned home, his wife asked where he had gone. He replied that he had gone to earn money. The wife rebuked him, 'What a strange fellow you are! Our son is dead. His death rites are to be performed. And you left us in such misery.'

The man said, 'don't forget that one day I saw a beautiful dream. I saw my seven sons. We were living happily. You disturbed me calling me ? I could not see any of my dream-children. But I did not feel sad then, so why should I feel sorry for this child?'

This body is like a rented house. We pay our bills through disease, loss, misery and sorrows. We live in the world as long as we have to pay the rent. Once the rent is paid we have to quit the world.

Hence give up the obsession with 'I and 'mine'. Surrender completely to the supreme soul so that you will attain liberation. Ego is really a narrow and dangerous thought. This ego remains as long as the body is there. It degrades one. There is a saying, 'If wishes were horses beggars would ride them.' Dreams are false, unreal, imaginary and illusory. Hence Lord Krishna advises us in the *Gita* that after our dream is shattered everything around us appear false. It is wisdom and awakening only which take away the illusion of birth and death as wakefulness removes ignorance.

●

Verse – 24

त्वयि मयि चान्यत्रैको विष्णुः व्यर्थं कुप्यसि मय्यसहिष्णुः ।
भव समचित्तः सर्वत्र त्वं वाञ्छस्यचिराद्यदि विष्णुत्वम् ।।
भज गोविन्दम् ।। २४ ।।

Meaning – Lord Vishnu is present everywhere. Why do you get angry with me? If you wish to be Vishnu, then leave off your sense of distinctions and keep still.

Commentary – In the *Gita* it is pointed out how God is present in all entities. He is the cause of the whole creation. In the it is said,

ईश्वरः सर्वभूतानां हृद्देशेऽर्जुन तिष्ठति ।
भ्रामयन् सर्वभूतानि यन्त्ररूढानि मायया ।। (18 / 61)

The Lord is present in the heart of everything. He controls all events and moves and directs all.

God is the source of such illusion. That illusion binds the whole creation. A snake has poison, which never harms it but it harms others. So also illusion binds all creatures in worldly troubles.

The next sloka in the same chapter says -

तमेव शरणं गच्छ सर्वभावेन भारत ।
तत् प्रसादात् परां शान्तिं स्थानं प्राप्स्यसि शाश्वतम् ।। (18 / 62)

The Lord addresses Arjun and says, 'You have to

surrender to God. If God blesses you, you can attain eternal peace. It does not mean that we have to leave worldly life. If all quit the world how the creation will progress? When one cuts a jackfruit, one has to oil one's palm so that the gum of the fruit wont stick. Some fish live in mud, but when they come out of the pond, there is no dirt on their bodies. Likewise, while working in the world, a man can remain detached. One can attach one's mind to God like water particles, which cannot wet the lotus leaf.

It is not possible to see the sky in its entirety. We can see only the sky at the horizon. We feel awed by looking at the vantness and grandness of the sky. In fact, the sky is only void. As long as we have a physical entity we cannot fathom the ethereal divinity. When we fail to comprehend the sky, how can we realize God? It is easy to see him as an incarnation in human form. In fact, God is omniscient, omnipresent and omnipotent. He is true, benevolent and beautiful. He is the store-house of all virtues.

Hiranyakashipu once asked his son Prahlad 'I am your God. Who is greater than me in this world?' Prahlad replied, 'God is omnipresent. He is verily present in me, in you, in flora and fauna.' Hiranya got angry with his son and asked him, pointing to the pillar in front of him, 'Is your God inside this pillar?' Prahlad said emphatically 'Yes'. Hiranya struck the pillar and God appeared assuming a strange form : half man and half lion. He killed the non-believer. Likewise God always listens to one who prays earnestly. God listens to one's prayer but it does not mean that God will fulfill all our wishes. A thief prays to God to steal someone's wealth without any obstruction. A hunter prays to God to hunt a deer successfully. A player, an examinee, a businessman – all pray to God to achieve their goals. Is it that God will listen to all the prayers? If he fulfils desires of everyone then this beautiful creation will turn ugly. God is benign, merciful and kind. He knows the past, the present and the future. His performance is to give justice to all the creatures. A real devotee should pray not for his selfish ends but for the benefit of the whole creation. Hence we should pray for the well-being of everyone :

सर्वे भवन्तु सुखिनः सर्वे सन्तु निरामयाः ।
सर्वे भद्राणि पश्यन्तु मा कश्चित् दुःखभाग् भवेत् ।।

One day, a monk was passing through a forest. He felt tired. He prayed to God to give him a horse. He immediately saw a horse in front of him. He got a creeper and made a rein. When he was about to sit on the horse, he saw the female horse delivering a calf. The monk could not go away. The mother horse did not move leaving her baby. Hence the monk held the calf. He said to God, 'O'God, what did you give me? Instead of helping me you have placed a burden on me. I could not ride the horse, rather, it is riding me.'

Those who are disillusioned suffer like this monk. People expect a life free from burden but they really suffer from misery. Their prayer is not answered. In such a condition they feel mentally disturbed. Who are to be considered steady and conscientious? In the *Gita* it is said -

प्रजहाति यदा कामान् सर्वान् पार्थ मनोगतान् ।
आत्मन्येवात्मना तुष्टः स्थितप्रज्ञस्तदोच्यते ।। (2 / 55)

One who has quitted desires, and is absorbed in divine thoughts is genuinly calm and quiet. He is really wise.

●

Verse – 25

शत्रौ मित्रे पुत्रे बन्धौ मा कुरु यत्नं वग्रहसन्धौ ।
सर्वस्मिन्नपि पश्यात्मानं सर्वत्रोत्सृज भेदाज्ञानम् ।।
भज गोविन्दम् ।। २५।।

Meaning – Don't waste your energy in loving or hating your kids, relations, friends or foes. Pay equal attention to all. Remove the sense of distinction from your mind if it is there out of ignorance. Then only can one see the supreme soul.

Commentary – Whether it is friendship or enmity, it increases attachment. Sorrows result from this attachment. Unless one keeps away from illusion and attachment one cannot attain salvation. This is why we have to see all as equals and realize that God is present in every being. Narrow-mindedness and distinctions put obstruction on the path to salvation. Hence instead of involving oneself in friendship and hostility one has to concentrate on the Supreme Soul. Brahman is in my body, in your body and in all creatures. In the *Gita* it is said,

उद्धरेदात्मनात्मानं नात्मानमवसादयेत् ।
आत्म्यैव ह्यात्मनो बन्धुरात्म्यैव रिपुरात्मनः ।। (6 / 5)

God says 'Don't fall down, because you are your friend and you are your enemy.' A conscientious man leads his mind as its friend and an unwise person's mind becomes his foe. Lord Krishna says this to Arjun in the next sloka,

बन्धुरात्मात्मनस्तस्य येनात्म्यैवात्मना जित: ।
अनात्मनस्तु शत्रुत्वे वर्त्तेतात्म्यैव शत्रुवत् ।। (6 / 6)

One who has conquered one's own self lives peacefully. Such a one does not bother about praise or disgrace. This type of man achievers divinity.

Man is responsible for his own ups and downs. He creates his own friend or enemy. Nobody else is required for one's well-being nor for one's fall. One has to accept the mind of a disciple and remove all kinds of differences from one's mind otherwise a spiritual teacher cannot do anything. What is the necessity of delicious food if there is no hunger ?

One is one's own friend, until there is no feeling of 'self' and 'mine'.

A man who enjoys worldly life harms oneself. In the *Bhagabad Gita* it is said -

आत्मौपम्येन सर्वत्र समं पश्यति योऽर्जुन ।
सुखं वा यदि वा दु:खं स योगी परमो मत: ।। (6/32)

Lord Krishna says, 'Oh Arjun! The devotee who sees me like his own body everywhere and remains indifferent to his sorrows and joys is really a great saint.'

A common man sees himself in his body. He takes equal care of all the parts of his body, so does a devotee who sees God in himself, who is present equally in all other creatures. He tries to remove sorrows of all and tries to give pleasure to all. He does not boast of his efficiency or of his belongings. Rather he attributes all his achievements to God. As the mother Ganges is worshipped with her own water, as the Sun God is worshipped with his own light, so also a devotee worships his Lord with the materials gifted by him. In *Bhaktisahityam*, it is said -

त्वदीयं वस्तु गोविन्दं तुभ्यमेव समर्पये ।

A real devotee sees the supreme soul as one with all souls, he also sees his own body as the same as that of others. Therefore, he feels sad when others experience sorrows and feels elated when others rejoice. Real humanity consists in not feeling sad thinking of others' sorrows. One must try to remove others' troubles. There is a moral in the Upanishads–

यस्तु सर्वाणि भूतानि आत्मन्येवानुपश्यति ।
सर्वभूतेषु चात्मानं ततो न विजुगुप्सते ।।

'One who sees all in himself and himself in all creatures never hates anybody nor ignores anybody.'

There was an illiterate rustic villager who took his son to a pandit. He requested the teacher to educate his son. The teacher was merciful towards the man. So he agreed. The boy came to his house daily and swept the dirt from the teacher's house. One day the boy found the teacher alone. He requested him to teach him something valuable. Just before this the teacher had a discussion with another intellectual. He said at once, you repeat 'Aham Brahmarshi' - it means 'I am the supreme soul'.

The boy came back home feeling happy. He repeated. 'Aham Brahmarshi'. His father asked him, 'Tell my son, what is the meaning of these two words?' The boy did not know the meaning. Hence his father said, 'I am Brahma'. Then the boy recited – My father is Brahma. The next day he went to his uncle's house. His uncle said, your father is not Brahma,

'I am Brahma'.

The boy was confused. He knew that his father might commit mistakes but his intelligent uncle won't. Hence he got this by heart : 'I am Brahma means, my uncle is Brahma'.

While reciting thus the boy came back home. On the way he met the headman of the village who laughed and said, 'O boy, I am Brahma' does not mean that your uncle is Brahma. It means 'I am Brahma.'

The boy got more confused. He sat at the outskirts of the village and pondered the question, 'How is it that his father is Brahma, his uncle is Brahma and his village head is also Brahma?'

Meanwhile the sun set. The night passed and it was dawn. The boy kept reciting the same line. Gradually, an awakening took place in his mind. He could realize the real meaning of those two words. He found his father, uncle, village headman and all others in the world were Brahma or the Supreme Soul.

In the *Gita,* it is said,

विद्याविनयसंपन्ने ब्राह्मणे गवि हस्तिनि ।
शुनि चैव श्वपाके च पण्डिता: समदर्शिन: ।। (5 / 18)

It means that wise people find the same Supreme Soul in the humble Brahmin, in a sweeper, in a cow, or an elephant or a dog. Hence the Supreme Soul is eternal and universal.

Verse – 26

कामं क्रोधं लोभं मोहं त्यक्त्वाऽत्मानं पश्यति सोऽहम् ।
आत्मज्ञानविहीना मूढास्ते पच्यन्ते नरकनिगूढा: ।।
भज गोविन्दम् ।। २६ ।।

Meaning – Think deeply about the question 'who am I ?' Leave attachment, desires, anger and greed, which are one's enemies. Engage in introspection and a search for soul. A man without the knowledge of the self is really a foolish man. Such people suffer a lot and are hell-bound.

Commentary - Lord Krishna has said in the *Gita* -

दम्भो दर्पोऽभिमानश्च क्रोध पारुष्यमेव च ।
अज्ञानं चाभिजातस्य पार्थ सम्पदमासुरीम् ।। (16 / 4)

It means – O' Arjun, a man's pride, ego, anger, sternness and unreasonableness are demonic qualities.

Krishna reiterates it in another sloka-

त्रिविधं नरकस्येदं द्वारं नाशनमात्मन: ।
काम: क्रोधस्तथा लोभस्तस्मादेतत् त्रयं त्यजेत् ।। (16 / 21)

To say that desire, anger and greed save the path to hell. These are responsible for the downfall of a man. Hence it is best to renounce such things.

The great sage Biswamitra's anger provides us with a fitting example. Biswamitra was the king in the Tretaya Yuga. One day, he started to conquer the world. There was a dense forest. His army was tired. He came accross the hermitage of another great sage, Vasistha. Vasistha greeted them as he found them in trouble. But how to treat the king and his great army? In his hermitage there was the cow Nandini. Vasistha loved her as his daughter. She comforted the sage and assured him the king would receive proper hospitality. She made all arrangements for the food and lodging of the king and his army.

The next day the king took farewell from the sage. He asked the former how such excellent hospitality could be provided to him and his army in a forest at night. The sage praised the cow for whom all such arrangements for the guests were possible. The king felt greedy. He desired to take that cow Nandini to his palace. As the sage did not agree to spare the benevolent cow the king ordered his army to take the cow forcibly. Nandini was watching from a distance. Basistha was very sad and has rolled down his cheeks. Nandini could not bear him to see him suffer, so she shook her tail and there emerged thousands of soldiers who defeated the army of king Biswamitra. The king felt deeply humiliated. He planned revenge.

King Biswamitra prayed to Lord Shiva, who, satisfied with his austerity gave him weapons. He went to Basistha and used hurled these at the sage but to no avail as the sage had a brahmastra, the most powerful weapon. Biswamitra felt more insulted. Again, he practised severe austerities to get that powerful weapon. Lord Brahma gave him the weapon 'brahmadanda' and conferred the title of 'brahmarshi' – the enlightened sage. Lord Brahma said, 'Now Vasistha will address you as 'brahmarshi'. If he does not pay you proper respects then you come back and he will be burnt alive'.

Biswamitra, now swollen with pride, went straight to the hermitage of Vasistha. From a distance, when Vasistha called him Rajarshri, his anger knew no bound. He suspected that Brahma might have cheated him. If he would back Vasistha, he must be burnt alive. But he restrained himself. He thought that he could not become a 'brahmarshi' practising such austerities, why should he burn a 'brahmarshi'. I may not be a 'brahmarshi' but I should never show my back to Vasistha. He walked backwards. Vasistha was pleased to see a great change in Viswamitra. Hence he called him 'brahmarshi'.

There is another story about greed. Greed is the source of all sins. There was a miserly man whose wife was a saintly woman. If any beggar came to their house the man used to shout at him and drive him away. One day, he was a way from home. At that time, a saintly person came to his house. The woman took good care of him. When the guest took leave of her, she said that her husband was too greedy, hence she was worried how his nature would be changed?

The saint said, 'You pretend that you are sick and the medicine has been prescribed by a saint, who had come to their house, it was 'papara bapa' meaning the father of sin. If she would not take the medicine she would die in two days.'

The man loved his wife. He ran to the medicine shop but no such medicine could be found there. One prostitute lived upstairs. She heard about the medicine. She called him, and said, 'Come to me, I have that medicine'.

The man was in a fix. On one hand, his beloved wife was ill and on the other, his own prestige was at stake. The prostitute showed him a ten rupee note and said, 'Take this money along with medicine'.

The man was greedy, hence he was axcited at the prospect of getting money. He went upstairs. The prostitute offered him a seat. As he was reluctant, she forcibly put the note inside his pocket. Then she offered him food. He declined telling her that he was of the Brahmin caste and she was a fallen woman. Then she gave a fifty rupee note to him and requested to take at least water from her. He agreed. Then she gave a hundred rupee note and requested him to let her make him drink. The greedy man accepted her offer. The woman said, 'Thank God, all sins from my previous birth have been washed out'. Then she requested him to take some food so that she would be released from a sinful life. Saying this she gave him two hundred rupee notes. The man agreed when he received more money. Finally she gave him a five-hundred rupee note and requested him to let her feed him. He agreed and she put him on her lap. As soon as he opened his mouth she slapped hard and said, This is called the 'father of sins'. She said, 'You were talking of sin, but agreed to accept my money out of greed. This is the result of desire and greed.'

Another interesting story is related here. Once upon a time there was a king. He felt uneasy for the sycophants who surrounded him. He was worried about how to get rid of worldly cares. Fortunately, a wise man came to his court. He delivered lectures on scriptures, but the king could not understand the deep philosophy behind the lessons. The king asked him to tell him how he could be free from attachments. The wise man could not give an answer. Hence the king said, 'If you cannot give the answer to my question you will be beheaded after two days.'

The wise man came back home feeling dejected. The first day passed in sorrow. The next day was the last day in his life. He broke down and cried. His daughter asked the reason of his sorrows. He narrated what had happened to him. The girl requested him to take her to the court. She assured him, 'I will tell the king how he could free himself from the world full of attachments.'

The wise man took his daughter to the court. He went on giving sermons, suddenly the girl embraced a pillar near her and cried loudly. She asked everyone to save her from the grip of the pillar. The king was worried seeing the girl crying. He shouted at her, 'Why are you crying to save you from the grip of the pillar? You have embraced it yourself. This is very strange.'

The girl laughed. The king asked why she was laughing. She said, 'Sir, you are the king. I am laughing because of your foolishness. You want to learn from my father about the way to get liberated from worldly attachments. You yourself cling to the world. You have not forsaken your greed for power, wealth, your pride, vanity and attachment to your wife, children and your kith and kin. When you loosen your ties with all these and hold God tight then only you can find ways of liberating yourself. It lies within you, why do you search for it outside?'

The king realized his mistake and achieved self-knowledge.

In all the above stories one gets lessons on the evil effects of desire. Regarding the attainment of knowledge of the self in the *Gita,* Lord Krishna says,

आपूर्यमाणमचलं प्रतिष्ठं
समुद्रमापः प्रविशन्ति यद्वत् ।

तद्वत् कामा यं प्रविशन्ति सर्वे
स शन्तिमाप्नोति न कामकामी ।। (2/70)

It means that a wise man is never disturbed amidst all sorts of entertainment like the ocean which keeps cool in spite of water from various rivers pouring into it. That man is blessed when he renounces everything in life. A man full of desires and aspirations cannot be happy. Hence Krishna in the *Gita* says-

विहाय कामान्यः सर्वान्पुमांश्चरति निःस्पृहः ।
निर्ममो निरहंकारः स शान्तिमधिगच्छति ।। (2/71)

Only he who has given up ego, desires and attachment can lead a quiet and peaceful life.

●

Verse – 27

गेयं गीतानामसहस्त्रं ध्येयं श्रीपतिरूपमजस्त्रम् ।
नेयं सज्जनसङ्गे चित्तं देयं जीनजनाय च वित्तम् ।।
भज गोविन्दम् ।। २७ ।।

Meaning – Read *Bhagabad Gita* and recite the name of Vishnu regularly. Meditate on Vishnu, the consort of Sri Laxhmi. Spend your time in the company of holy persons. Donate whatever you want to the needy and the poor.

Commentary – The slokas from 14 to 27 are included in *'Chaturdiga Manjarika'* which were composed by his followers when Shankar went on a pilgrimage to Kashi.

There are four lessons on how to spend one's spiritual life in order to attain self-knowledge *(atma gyaana)*. These are – concentration on the *Gita,* worship of Sri Narayan, company of sages and gifts. These lessons are given in all scriptures. In the 20th verse the essence of the *Gita* has been discussed at length. One, who reads the *Gita,* is never touched by any sin and he floats like a lotus leaf which does not became wet by water. It is said in the *Mahabharat* –

महापापादिपापानि गीताध्यानं करोति चेत् ।
क्वचित् स्पर्शं न कुर्वन्ति नलिनीदलमम्बुवत् ।।

The *Gita* is an extraordinary scripture. Nobody has fully understood it. Through deep study new ideas and meanings emerge. With our limited wisdom we cannot grasp the essential inner meaning of the lessons deliberated in the *Gita*. Even if our wisdom grasps it, our mind fails to retain it. Even the mind cannot express what it has learnt. If one tries to express it our words fail to convey it. That is why the *Gita* is full of limitless wisdom.

The *Gita* is the essence of all the Upanishads because the theory contained in the *Gita* is more valuable. The *Vedas* are the breath of Lord Vishnu and the *Gita* contains His words. All philosophy is included in the *Gita* but it does not belong to any philosophy. The *Gita* does not support any idealism. This scripture is really wonderful. One who desires to help oneself, should read the *Gita* and get attracted to it, no matter what caste, creed or religion he belongs to.

It is said,

मूकं करोति वाचालं पङ्गुं लङ्घयते गिरिम् ।
यत्कृपा तमहं वन्दे परमानन्दमाधवम् ।। *(Gita Dhyanam)*

If a man receives divine mercy he can speak in spite of his dumbness and a lame man can scale a mountain. Hence the *Gita* is like a boat by means of which one can cross the ocean of this world.

संसारसागरं घोरं तर्त्तुमिच्छति यो नरः ।
गीतानावं समासाद्य पारं याति सुखेन सः ।।

(Subhasita Ratna Bhandaram)

9th to the 13th verses advise us to keep good company. There is a story narrating the consequences of keeping bad company. There was a painter in Rome. He was searching for a man who must be simple, beautiful, sinless and lively.

He came across a boy at the end of the lane. The artist found what he was searching for. He invited the boy and drew his picture while he was sitting on his veranda. After finishing the painting he gave one copy to the boy. That art was so life-like that it was sold at a high price. The artist earned a lot from this painting.

One day he thought that he would draw the picture of a selfish, hypocritical and cunning person. In order to find such an evil person he went to a jail. He was satisfied with the appearance of a particular culprit. As soon as he disclosed his plan to him, the culprit shouted at him. When he offered to pay him a sum of money he agreed to his proposal. The artist told him that he would not only give him money but also a copy of his best painting. After the job was done according to the jail practice, money was deposited with the jailor and the painting of the child was given to the prisoner.

The prisoner looked at the picture. Tears flowed down his cheeks. After some time he said 'This picture was painted when I was a child.' It is better to live in hell than to live with bad people. I suffer because of such bad company. The great economist and moralist Chanakya advises us to forsake bad company.

दुर्जन: परिहर्त्तव्यो विद्ययालंकृतोऽपि सन् ।
मणिना भूषित: सर्प: किमसौ न भयङ्कर: ।।

In this sloka, along with meditation and keeping good company, one is also advised to serve the poor. The *Vedas*, do not denounce earning wealth. In the second sloka one is urged not to be attached to wealth. After earning money one should not guard it always like a snake. Wealth should be liberally distributed. This is the Vedic financial rule. It is said, 'Money is like manure. It you spread it around, it does a lot of good. But if you pile it up in one place it stinks like hell.' Hence, it is to be understood that the price of wealth lies not in depositing it but in giving it away. The great king Harsabardhan gave all his wealth away once in every five years. He offered his clothes to the needy and covered himself with a piece of cloth given to him by his sister, Rajashree. The traveller Huensang wrote about his charitable deeds in his travelogue. So great was Indian culture.

All the money we earn should be divided into five parts. The first part is meant for spiritual work. The second should be set apart for the country. The third part is to be invested in trade and business. The fourth is meant for one's family and the fifth part should be given to your relatives. When wealth is given away it increases, it never decreases. Sage Kabir and the *Rig Veda* stress the benefits of charity and the bad effects of hoarding money. Kabir says -

चिडीचोञ्च भर ले गयि, नदी न घटता नीर ।
दान दिये धन ना घटे, कह गये भगत कवीर । *(Kabir Doha)*

In *Yajurveda Brahman,* it is said -

मोघमन्नं विन्दति अप्रचेता सत्यं व्रवीमि वध इत्स तस्य ।
नार्यमणं पुष्यति नो सखायं केवलाघो भवति केवलादी ।।

It means that one who enjoys all his wealth himself his possession of money is useless because it becomes the cause of his death. He only accumulates sin.

Lord Ramachandra descends from the dynasty of king Raghu. After the completion of sacrificial worship Raghu donated all his wealth. One day he was sitting quietly. An ascetic came to him and begged for fourteen potfuls of gold. He said, 'My preceptor has asked this much from me.'

Raghu was worried. He said, 'Now I own only what I wear. My treasury is empty. How can I get so much gold?'

Raghu pondered for some time and then wrote a letter to Kubera, the Lord of wealth. The Lord read the letter and rejected his appeal outright. He said 'Let Raghu fight with me. If he wins he will get whatever he desires'. As soon as Raghu learnt this from the ascetic he prepared himself for the battle. He held weapons and prepared to attack Kubera. The Lord actually did not want to fight with Raghu, hence he allowed him to enter his kingdom.

Kubera laughed and said to Raghu, 'My kingdom is sanctified receiving the dust of your feet. Hence you can take as much wealth as you need.' Kubera desired to set his eyes on Raghu, the generous one.

The ascetic got gold from Raghu. He paid his dues to his master.

In the *Rig Veda* it is said how ill-got money cannot help one at one's hour of need-

न ता न शान्ति न भाति तस्करो
नासामामित्रो व्यथीरो दधर्षति ।
देवांश्च यभिर्यजते ददाति च
ज्योगित्ताभि: सचते गेपति: सह ।।

It means that money earned by evil means can never

help one. The wealth acquired by theft and murder cannot be useful. Neither the donor nor the receiver can attain salvation.

Hence it is said,

न दातुं नोपभोक्तुं च शक्नोति कृपणः श्रियम् ।
किन्तु स्पृशति हस्तेन नपुंसक इव स्त्रियम् ।। (Mahabharat)

A miser is compared with a eunuch. A eunuch can touch a woman but cannot enjoy her. So also a miserly man can only see wealth but cannot enjoy it.

Hence sage Bhartrihari has said in *Nitishatakam*,

दानं भोगो नाशस्तिस्त्रो गतयो भवन्ति वित्तस्य ।
यो न ददाति न भुङ्क्ते तस्य तृतीया गतिर्भवति ।।

One who earns money and spends it on charity is acclaimed everywhere. All wealth has three uses – donation, enjoyment and destruction. One who cannot donate it nor can spend it properly, his money gets wasted. It is sacrifice of money not enjoyment that is appreciated in all ages. No donor becomes poor. If money is donated to a deserving person, then such wealth is properly used and it increases. On the other hand if it is misused then the wealth is lost. One who never sacrifices his wealth is considered a cruel-hearted man. Nobody feels sympathy for such a cruel and miserly man.

The Goddess of wealth, Laxhmi, is restless. For her quick movement one who is wealthy today may turn into a poor man on some other day. One who is a pauper today may become a millionaire. As wealth is a fleeting entity, it should be used properly. One can earn fame and peace with such use of one's property. One loses mental peace when money is ill-spent. The hoarded money in a store-house is like stone.

In *Hitopadesh* it is said,

धनानि जीवितं चैव परार्थे प्राज्ञः उत्सृजेत् ।
सन्निमित्ते वयं त्यागो विनाशे नियेत सति ।।

A wise man renounces wealth and life for the benefit of others. As wealth and life are perishable, both should be renounced for a noble purpose.

●

Verse – 28

सुखतः क्रियते रामाभोगः पश्चाद्धन्तः शरीरे रोगः ।
यद्यपि लोके मरणं शरणं तदपि न मुञ्चति पापाचरणम् ।।
भज गोविन्दम् ।। २८ ।।

Meaning – A man takes recourse to physical pleasure while searching for happiness. In fact, such carnal pleasures invite diseases. In spite of knowing that death is inevitable, a man cannot give up his sinful actions. This is a matter of regret.

Commentary – Those who are intensely engaged in mundane pleasures find it quite difficult to conquer their desires. Even in old age they cannot abandon the habit of indulging in sensual pleasures. One has to give up worldly pleasures in order to attain real happiness. Jajati, the great king, spent his youth and then borrowed his son's youth and enjoyed the company of Devjani but could not find satiety. What he learnt from his life he commnicated one day to his wife through the tale of a goat couple.

Once a goat came near a well when he searched for food. He saw that a female goat had fallen into the well. He tried to help her by digging the earth. Finally he rescued her. She showed her gratitude and expressed her desire to marry him. Many other she-goats desired to marry the same goat for his handsomeness. The goat got attracted towards them and enjoyed them all. The she-goat who was rescued from the well could not tolerate his adultery. So she returned to her master. But the goat pursued her. On the way he persuaded her to comeback to him but without success. The master of the she-goat was a Brahmin. He learnt from her about the goat's licentiousness and punished him by chopping his private parts. As he was the protector of her life, she requested her master to undo the effects of the severe punishment. The Brahmin again connected his organ using his yogic powers and the goat went on enjoying his consort.

Shukracharya was the teacher of the demons. His daughter was Devjani. The daughter of the demon king Brushaparva was Sharmistha. One day both the girls were taking bath in a pond. Lord Shiva appeared there with His consort Parbati. Sharmistha in a hurry wore the garment of Devjani. Devjani picked up a quarrel with her. Sharmitha got angry with Devjani. She snatched her dress and pushed her into the well. King Jajati arrived there and saw the girl crying inside the well. He gave her clothes as she was naked and rescued her from the well. Jajati got married to Devjani and Sharmitha had to serve her in their palace as a penance for her misdeed. Sharmistha was extremely beautiful. Hence Jajati kept up an illicit relationship with her. Both Sharmitha and Devjani got pregnant and each gave birth to children. Devjani got annoyed with Jajati and went back to her father's place.

Shukracharya got aggrieved and cursed Jajati to suffer from premature ageing. After Jajati prayed to Shukracharya to forgive him, he was given the chance to get back his youth on the condition that if anybody willingly opted for his old age he would get back his youth. Nobody accepted such a proposal. Finally it was Puru, the youngest son of Sharmistha, who agreed. Jajati got his son's youth and spent many days with Devjani happily. Still then his sexual urge was not satiated.

The king became aware of his situation. He said to his wife that he was like that goat. He had exchanged his old age with his son's youth. After indulging in pleasure so long now he realized that he had forgotton the goal of his life. When ghee is poured into a fire it burns with a stronger flame, so also the sense organs grow more demanding if they are not suppressed. Eastern people follow western life-styles without rhyme and reason. J. Mechinji has rightly commented, 'Desire the thirst which finds pleasure in objects or craves for the satisfaction of needs, is the root of suffering.'

Sensuous man goes through the cycles of lives like monkeys which jump from one tree to another. His desires are never satisfied. A man subject to sensuousness suffers from misery. Drinking salty water enhances thirst. Desire deceives one like the mirage in a desert. The 'Sankhya Joga' chapter in the *Gita* explains how a man, trying to give satisfaction to any sense organs suffers a lot.

Once sage Vyasadeva said to his disciple, Jaimini,

बलवान् इन्द्रियग्रामो विद्वांसं नापकर्षति ।।

It means that sense organs are always powerful. They make even wise people take wrong steps. Jaimini did not accept this advice. He said that he had conquered all sorts of desire. He twisted the sloka and said,

बलवान् इन्द्रियग्रामो विद्वांसमपि कर्षति । *(Manu Smruti 2-20)*

it menas that sensuous pleasures cannot distract wise men. Vyasadev did not agree, so he kept quiet.

After a few days, in the evening when all the residents of the hermitage were busy meditating, a sudden storm of rain lashed the place. A beautiful woman arrived. She was completely drenched. Her body parts were visible. She requested the young monk Jaimini to give her shelter in his cottage. He agreed. The woman took off her clothes and tried to dry it in the sacrificial fire. The sage could not control himself at the sight of the naked woman. He expressed his desire to enjoy her. She put a condition that he had to carry her on his shoulder and move around the sacrificial fire for three times. The sage did the same but before the end of the third round the woman landed a heavy blow on his head and shouted that wise people also can go astray. Jaimini was surprised to hear the truth. When he looked up, he saw his own spiritual preceptor instead of the woman. He felt offended. He repented for his mistake and saluted his teacher with great reverence. He finally admitted saying **'विद्वांसमपि कर्षति'** ।

बलवान् इन्द्रियग्रामो विद्वांसमपि कर्षति ।

Sometimes wise men also fall a victim to sensuousness.

●

Verse – 29

अर्थमनर्थं भावय नित्यं नास्ति ततः सुखलेशः सत्यम् ।
पुत्रादपि धनभाजां भीतिः सर्वत्रैषा विहिता रीतिः ।।
भज गोविन्दम् ।। २९ ।।

Meaning – Wealth is the root cause of all misery. That wealth cannot impart happiness is a universal truth. A rich man loses his faith and confidence even in his son on account of this wealth. This is seen everywhere in all ages.

Commentary – In the second sloka the seeker of truth has been warned against possession of wealth. He is advised instead to be satisfied with his own earnings. In the eleventh sloka he is advised not to boast of wealth, family and youth as these are ephemeral. In the thirteenth sloka it is said that only noble company can give security to one who lives in this mundane world of attachments. In the seventeenth chapter the seeker is advised to donate generously instead of amassing wealth. In this sloka it is explained how the above said lessons, if not followed, cause disaster in family relationships.

To susbtantiate such statements three interesting stories have been narrated here.

Once two friends were passing through a jungle. They met a sage who was running. He was shouting, 'I am not scared of death, nor of tiger and lion. I am afraid of wealth as it only can devastate most in worldly life.' The two friends could not believe all this. They advanced further and met four burglars on the way. They held two packets of gold and money. They were enjoying themselves while laughing to their hearts content. The chief of the thieves felt hungry. He sent two of his followers to the market to fetch some food. Meanwhile the chief along with the other thief planned to kill those two who had gone for food, so that they two would get more money.

The thieves who went to get food, also planned to kill the chief and their friend. So they added poison to their food and came to the chief. But as soon as they arrived, the chief and his follower stabbed them with a sharp knife and they died instantly.

The chief and his follower merrily took the poisoned food thinking of the larger share of the money both of them would have. But after taking the food both succumbed to death.

Thus due to avarice and adoption of foul means, none of them could enjoy wealth. Now the two friends realized that what the sage was telling was really true. There is nothing more dangerous than wealth.

The second story is about a widow who was quite wealthy. She had a son who was growing up in luxury. As he grew older his misdeeds also cropped up. The abundant paternal property was the root cause of his bad qualities. Many people came to him for his wealth as frogs flock to a pond full of water. Evil-minded people rather than good ones came to him in greater number. Slowly they got him to adopt bad habits. Under the influence of such friends he needed money more and more and demanded it from his mother. His mother felt worried about the changes in the boy. She did not want to see his face. Everybody in the neighbourhood mocked at her. Family prestige was brought down. The mother thought that whether such a spoilt child lived or died ment nothing to her. So she put poison in his food. The boy also planned to remove his mother from his desired path.

A time came when the son hit the mother's head with an iron rod as a result she collapsed on the floor. Then the boy took the food his mother had prepared and died as it was poisoned. Thus the craving for wealth resulted in the death of both mother and son.

The third story is more interesting. Once upon a time there was a landlord who had vast landed property. A certain poor labourer was working in his house. Earning only five rupees in a day he looked quite happy. He spent his day merrily with his wife and children. But the rich man always felt worried about his wealth. His wife look notice of this and asked her husband. 'How was it that the labourer with so little income looked so happy?'

The landlord tried to play a trick. He kept ninety nine rupees in a bag and put it inside the labourer's room.

The wife of the labourer came across the bag. She gave it to her husband. He found that it contained money. They counted and found one rupee less than one hundred. Hence he suggested that they take food without fries. They took only curry and saved money thereby. Their motive was to make it hundred by saving money.

Gradually their savings amounted to one hundred and fifty rupees. The labourer got encouraged to save more. Hence they began taking rice with onion and salt without curry.

This money he now invested and got interest. Thus the amount of money increased but his peace of mind decreased. Children could not take milk. No delicious food was prepared on festive days. They could not find time for offering up prayers in the evening.

One day the landlord asked his wife how the labourer was getting on. The wife said that financially he was in a better condition but mentally he had become miserale. He did not laugh. He looked weak. He was taking dry bread. He was always sitting quiet.

The landlord said, this is called the trap of ninety-nine. One who is entrapped cannot find peace in life. The lessons from the *Bhagabata* are fittingly cited here -

अर्थस्य साधने सिद्धे उत्कर्षे रक्षणे व्यये ।
नाशोपभोग आयासस्त्रासश्चिन्ता भ्रमो नृणाम् ।।

स्त्रेयं हिंसाऽनृतं दम्भः कामः क्रोधः स्मयो मदः ।
भेदो वैरमविश्वासः संस्पर्धा व्यसनानि च ।।

एते पञ्चदशानर्थाः ह्यर्थमूला मता नृणाम् ।
तस्मादनर्थमर्थाख्यं श्रेयोऽर्थी दुरतस्त्यजेत् ।।

भिद्यन्ते भ्रातरो दारा पितर सुहृदस्तथा ।
एका स्निग्धाः काकिणिना सद्यः सर्वेऽरयः कृताः ।।

अर्थेनाल्पीयसा ह्येते संरब्धा दीप्तमन्यवः ।
त्यजन्त्याशु स्पृधो ध्वन्ति सहसोत्सृज्य सौहृदम् ।।

In order to accumulate money a man has to labour a lot and suffer from worries, fears and disillusionment. All sorts of sinful activities like theft, malice, falsefood, desire, anger, ego, enemity, loss of faith, alcoholism etc. are generated from avarice for wealth. That is why it is best to give up such harmful things. Because of this wealth one's own blood-relations like brothers, parents, wife and son turn enemies. For mere wealth disharmony results. Instead of love and affection everybody gets into quarrels. Due to disputes over wealth such conflicts arise that one does not hesitate to kill others. Thus attachment to wealth is discouraged as it invites calamities.

●

Verse – 30

प्राणायामं प्रत्याहारं नित्यानित्यविवेकविचारम् ।
जाप्यसमेतसमाधिविधानं कुर्ववधानं महदवधानम् ।।
भज गोविन्दम् ।। ३० ।।

Meaning – Try to attain *samaadhi* (total inner silence with perfect concentration) by performing *pranayam*, (regulation of breath) *pratyahar*, (withdrawal of senses) understanding of the differences between truth and falsehood, *japa* (recitation of God's name) and by performing meditation.

Commentary – In the previous slokas it has been suggested that one withdraws one's mind from alluring wealth and sexual enjoyment by means of which can one attain peace. Those were external activities. In this sloka Shankar has shown the path of inner spiritual practice. Eternal peace and happiness can be attained from within. We need not search for it outside.

Pranayam is controlled breathing practices. Pratyahar means control of the senses as a galloping horse's movements are controlled by pulling the rein. Pulling the senses inward is called pratyahar. These are very difficult to practice but easy to talk about. A spiritual seeker has to adopt some practices keeping himself in good company, studying scriptures, serving mankind with charity, self-control and regular spiritual activities.

About the importance of keeping good company it has been explained in the ninth, thirteenth and twenty-seventh verses. Scriptures like the *Veda,* the *Upanishad,* the *Gita,* the *Bhagabata,* the *Ramayan* and the *Mahabharat* are to be read attentively. The seeker has to analyse himself. The next principle is service. It is said, 'Service to mankind is service to God'. Hence one has to serve the poor, the helpless, the old and the sick. The next exercise concerns self-control. Our sense organs are like horses which draw the chariot of our body and our mind is like the charioteer. One has to distinguish between what is temporary and what is eternal and accordingly guide a horse and the charioteer. Never be a slave to the senses. The last principle is 'sadhana' or exercise. In the Gita it is said-

अपाने जुह्वति प्राणं प्राणेऽपानं तथा परे ।

प्राणापानगती रुद्ध्वा प्राणायाम परायणाः ।। (4 / 29)

Breath-controlling exercise is essential for developing as it refines one's physical, mental and spiritual energy. The life force and mind are closely connected. If somebody's mind is not fixed in meditation, this breath-controlling exercise can help him in order to keep mind quiet. Pranayam is not only breath-control but also a method of combining *pran* and *apan*. The control of one affects the other. Pranayam serves as a big bridge enabiling us to cross the ocean of worldly life. Hence in *Yoga Chudamani* it is said,

प्राणायामो भवेद्देवं पातकेन्धनपातकः ।

भवोदधिमहासेतुः प्रोच्यते योगिभिः सदा ।।

According to Patanjali, 'pratyahar' or withdrawal is the external part of Yoga. Sage Jagyanbalkya believes that pratyahar is the essence of yoga. According to him *'yama',* '*niyama*', '*asan*' and '*pranayam*' are the external parts and '*pratyahar*', '*dharana*', '*dhyan*' and '*samaadhi*' constitute the essence of Yoga.

One cannot get a good result out of pranayam or pratyahar unless one realizes the value of life. Hence it is necessary to know the difference between the permanent and the temporary. This is possible through meditation and good company. This helps in judiciously distinguishing the good from the bad, reality from illusion, the natural from the artificial and virtues from vices. To do so one has to act carefully. One has to give up one's interest in the self and surrender oneself to the creator of this world, then only can one attain divinity. Lord Krishna in the *Gita* says,

अनन्याश्चिन्तयन्तो मां ये जनाः पर्युपासते ।
तेषां नित्याभियुक्तानां योगक्षेमं वहाम्यहम् ।। (9/22)

One wise man was explaining this sloka to the king but the king was not satisfied with his interpretation. He ordered him to go back home and ponder over the meaning of the sloka, then come to him the next day.

The wise man came back home feeling offended. His wife took notice of the disgruntled look in his face. When he narrated that day's incident, his wife said, "The king is right; you have not interpreted the sloka properly'. The wise man felt more insulted and argued with his wife but no solution could be found.

The wife asked, 'Why did you go to the king? What was your motive?'

The wise man said, 'To support you and my family, otherwise why should I go there?'

This time his wife said politely, 'See, if you have realized the words of Sri Krishna you would have never gone to the king. If you had surrendered yourself to the Lord, you must worship him with full concentration; He would bear all your burden. You thought that the king would fulfill all your needs. You could not understand the essential meaning of the sloka; that is why the king was not satisfied with your answer.'

The wise man realized his mistake. Hence he did not go to the king. He engaged himself in prayer and meditation.

The king sent for the wise man. But the wise man said to the messenger, 'I am sorry for my mistake. Now I have surrendered myself to my Lord. I believe that He will fulfill all my needs.'

The messenger came back to the king and reported to him what he had heard. The king came to the wise man and fell at his feet. The wise man thanked the king and said, 'Thanks to you, I could realize my mistake. I am obliged to you.'

Verse – 31

गुरुचरणाम्बुजनिर्भरभक्तः संसारादचिराद्भव मुक्तः ।
सेन्द्रियमानसनियमादेवं द्रक्ष्यसि निजहृदयस्थदेवम् ।।
भज गोविन्दम् ।। ३१ ।।

Meaning – The teacher advises his disciples, 'You get liberated from worldly life by controlling your minds and sense organs. You can earn self-knowledge and behold the Lord soon.'

Commentary – The teacher is described in our scriptures as the creator, the sustainer and the destroyer.

गुरुर्ब्रह्मा गुरुर्विष्णुः गुरुर्देवमहेश्वरः ।
गुरुः साक्षात् परब्रह्म तस्मै श्रीगुरवे नमः ।।

Hence the help of the spiritual teacher is absolutely essential for one's progress along the right path. The story of Abadhuta and Jaduraja is narrated in *Srimad Bhagbad*. Abadhuta had twenty-four teachers. He showed how one can learn something from even the lowliest creatures. The earth is his first teacher. Like the earth, man likes to embrace works that creates suffering for him. The next teacher is the wind. He learns from the wind how to keep detached and treat all things as equal. The sun is a teacher who gives his rays to everyone without descriminating among them. He receives water and gives it back in the form of rain. A dove is another teacher, who gets too engrossed in worldly pleasures and as a result invites destruction.

A certain dove and his wife lived quite happily in a forest. One day, they left their young ones in a nest and flew away in search of food. Meanwhile a hunter came and put some grains on the floor and covered them with a net. The little birds were attracted towards this and fell into the net. On returning the dove couple found their nest empty. They were upset. They searched for the kids and found them inside the net. The mother dove could not control herself. She jumped into the net to reach her children but was herself entangled in it.

Hence one should learn a lesson from the she-dove's example about why one should keep one's mind under control. It is said, 'Look before you leap'. One should judiciously think prior to taking action.

Once Ramkrishna Paramahans told a story to his disciples. A certain farmer was sleeping in his cottage. Suddenly he woke up. He wanted to smoke. He came out with a lantern. He went to his friend who was sleeping in another room. He begged from him match sticks. The friend laughed and said, 'You are so foolish, you are not aware that you are holding the lantern from which you can light your cigarette.' The farmer realized his foolishness. The teacher shows us how to see God within ourselves. The *Gita* explains how to learn lessons from one's preceptor.

तद् विद्धि प्रणिपातेन परिप्रश्नेन सेवया ।
उपदेक्ष्यन्ति ते ज्ञानं ज्ञानिनस्तत्त्वदर्शिनः ।। (4 / 34)

Most of the people keep themselves engrossed in eating, sleeping, fear and copulation. All this is nothing but an illusion. One should search for a way to be rescued from such illusion.

For those who have lost their conscience and mind there is a lesson from 'the Bhagabata'.

न ते बिन्दुः स्वार्थगतिं हि विष्णुं
दुराशया ये बहिरर्थः मानिनः ।
अन्धा यथान्धैरूपनीयमाना-
स्तेऽपीशतन्त्र्यामुरुदाम्नि बद्धाः ।।

It means that, those who are engrossed in worldly life and accept a lustful man as their teacher, they don't know that Lord Vishnu is the only refuge. If one blind man follows another blindman he will certainly fall into a ditch. One should make sure that one does not fall down. Only a real teacher can save people who are bound by attachments.

There was a disciple who served his teacher honestly. He was proud of the service, he rendered. The teacher asked him to fetch some spices. The disciple got a black fruit of astringent taste. The teacher asked him to peel it. The poor fellow thought that the cover of the fruit is the outer skin, how can he offer to his teacher? He threw it away and gave the seed to his teacher. The teacher was annoyed with him. He said, 'O' foolish one, the outer skin of the fruit is edible, not its kernel.'

Another day the teacher asked the disciple to bring some spices after he finished his lunch. That day he got one black cardamom. He threw away all the seeds and presented the skin to his teacher. The teacher laughed at him. He explained to him how the same thing can be used as essential sometimes and can be rejected at some other time. Hence, in order to get real benefits from the two fruits one should not consider them as one and the same. The skin of one is not used whereas the skin of the other is much used. A spiritual preceptor explains such subtle differences between the objects. As a result, a student gets the benefit of gaining self-knowledge easily.

There was the hermitage of sage Dhoumya. His disciple was Upamanyu. He had no interest in studies. He did not pay attention to his teacher. But the teacher loved him very much. Slowly a change came over him. He was greedy for food. The teacher tried to make him get rid of this bad habit. He gave him a particular duty i.e. to lead the cattle to the forest during the day and return home with them in the evening. A food packet was given to him for his lunch. He was greedy person, so, it was not sufficient for him. Hence he drank the milk of the cows without taking the permission of his teacher. Gradually he looked fat. When the teacher asked him what he was eating in the forest, he told him the truth. The teacher explained to him how his action amounted to theft.

Upamanyu tried to find out another method for which he did not need the permission of the teacher. He took the drops of milk fallen from the teats of cow's udder. As the teacher came to know about what he did he took some unknown poisonous fruit. As a result he lost his eye-sight. He could not see, so he fell into a well.

It was dark, the cattle returned home but nowhere was Upamanyu to be seen. Hence the teacher went out a candle in hand, accompanied by some disciples in search of his student. He shouted 'Upamanyu', and got a response from the well. He came to him and taught him a 'mantra'. Upamanyu practiced that mantra. When he recited it Aswini

Kumar, the god of medicine, cured his eyes and he could see things again.

From that day Upamanyu refrained from sensuous indulgences and learnt wisdom from the teacher Dhoumya.

Human body can be compared to a kingdom. The name of the kingdom will be 'Binashpur' implying the decay of body. The name of the king of this kingdom is *'buddhi'* (intellect) and of the queen is *'mana'* (mind). The two ministers are *'raja'* and *'tama'*. The subjects of the kindom are calld the *'karmendriyas'* (kinetic sense organs) and the *'jynanendriyas'* (sense organs of wisdom). The hidden treasure inside the body is called *'Paramatma'* (The Supreme Soul).

When the body is ruled by mana or mind instead of budhi or intellect it tends to decay. Mind always moves swiftly. Hence, in order to keep it under control, intellect must be strict and guide it properly. Otherwise, mind will mislead one's conscience. Unless mind is controlled the rajas and the tamas energies will be invited to mislead a man. The sense organs controlled by mind will encourage one to go astray. The result is suffering.

Lord is settled in our bosom. If our mind is polluted He cannot express his divinity to us. Rajas and tamas rule over our conscience. Under the impact of greed, anger, illusion and attachments life becomes unbearable. It is only a true saint who can instruct one to move piously towards divinity. If qualities like rajas and tamas are removed from our whole being the sense organs will not put us in trouble. It results in turning the abode of destruction into the state of construction, which is undestructible.

Thus Acharya Shankar tries to convince all that in a perishable physique one can attain a perennial state.

Hence 'Bhaja Govindam',
Recite God's name.
Reiterate God's name.

Reference :

1. The Ramayan
2. The Mahabharat
3. Srimad Bhagabad Gita
4. The Bhagabata by Jagannath Das
5. Nitishatakam - Bhartrihari
6. Vairagya Shatakam - Bhartrihari
7. Bal Vikash - Sri Satyasai
8. Bhagabata Rasasagar - Gorachand Mishra
9. Upakatha Shatakam - Manoj Das
10. Rigveda Sourava - Priyabrata Das
11. Chirantani - Govinda Chandra Sahu
12. Sukta Shataka - Harihara Mishra
13. Manabodha Choutisha - Bhakta Charan Das
14. Vivek Chudamani - Sri Shankaracharya
15. Chanakya Nitisloka
16. The Essence of Sanatan Religion - Mohapatra Nilamani Sahu
17. Bhakti Yoga - Godabarisha Mohapatra
18. Pathachakra Diary - Chandra Sekhar Rath
19. Mahabharat Bichitra - Subodha Kumar Nanda
20. Kathopadesha - Srila Sandevananda Vidyabinod
21. Yaha Dhan Kiska Hai - Andand Swami Saraswati
22. Pourusha - a monthly magazine
23. The Samaj - daily newspaper
24. The Sambad - Daily newspaper
25. The times of India
26. Inspiring stories - Swami Sibananda